Thomasine Maunsell

Legends of the Jacobite wars

Katharine Fairfax, Isma O'Neil

Thomasine Maunsell

Legends of the Jacobite wars
Katharine Fairfax, Isma O'Neil

ISBN/EAN: 9783741103124

Manufactured in Europe, USA, Canada, Australia, Japa

Cover: Foto ©ninafisch / pixelio.de

Manufactured and distributed by brebook publishing software (www.brebook.com)

Thomasine Maunsell

Legends of the Jacobite wars

LEGENDS

OF THE

JACOBITE WARS.

LEGENDS

OF THE

JACOBITE WARS:

"KATHARINE FAIRFAX."—"ISMA O'NEIL."

BY

THOMASINE MAUNSELL.

"When civil dudgeon first grew high,
And men fell out, they knew not why;
When hard words, jealousies, and fears
Set folk together by the ears."

IN THREE VOLUMES.

VOL. III.

LONDON:
TINSLEY BROTHERS, 18, CATHERINE STREET, STRAND.
1873.

[*All Rights of Translation and Reproduction are reserved.*]

CHAPTER XXXII.

"Men tell me of truth now—False! I cry—
Of beauty—A mask friend! Look beneath!"
BROWNING.

THE short autumn evening was drawing to a close, and the dark shadows were gathering round the corners of the large sitting-room of Leagh Bawn. Now and then a fitful blaze from the wood-fire lit up the figures of the silent little group as they sat in the twilight, each occupied with her own thoughts. Mrs. Colthurst, half-dozing in her corner, speculated on the prospects of her son Frank, who was in the general way the beginning and end of all her meditations, while Grace, inwardly bemoaning the weary dulness of the times, was passing in mental review the chances and hopes which the future might unfold to her. Half in pity, half in scorn, she thought of Guy Henry, who she knew full well would lay down all he had at her feet; but what was it—nothing—nothing but an honest heart, and what was that to her? She could not give him back what he gave to her; she could not even understand the disinterested love which was a part of his nature. Far more akin to her feelings were the off-hand attentions of her last admirer. Lindesay Ward's clever sallies and insinuating manner, dazzled her fancy and left a more pleasing impression on her imagination. Guy was good no doubt, and an old friend, but how stupid compared with this new comer; and then she drew picture after picture in the fire-light, in which, as a matter of course, she formed the centre piece herself. Captain Ward's witty speeches were answered by repartees twice as clever as his own, and his captivation completed by a well-timed glance of those violet eyes, whose power she was by no means ignorant of.

Less brilliant were the pictures her

cousin Isma saw, as she sat gazing into the fire with a sad expression in her wide open grey eyes. Her present lonely, unsympathetic life only made her absent friends more dear to her, while the uncertainty of the future filled her with apprehension and anxiety. Would she ever see them again? and how? or where?

"There is surely some unusual noise downstairs: what can it be at this hour?" said Mrs. Colthurst suddenly rousing herself. "Isma, dear, do go and see: Grace is too sleepy to stir."

"I am not asleep I assure you, mother, but Isma wont mind going. Is any one arriving, do you think? Oh! for anything or anybody to bring us some life: I'm half dead with the stillness."

"Well, Isma, what is it?" she continued, as her cousin re-entered the room.

"Winny tells me a gentleman has just arrived, and it is some one you know, as he is coming up here."

"Who can it be?" said the young lady, rising with pleased alacrity.

"Frank perhaps, or your father," said Mrs. Colthurst, hurrying to the door.

"Oh dear no, mamma, it's only Guy. I know his voice," said Grace, sinking back again into her chair.

"Yes, it is 'only Guy.' You are right, Miss Colthurst," said that young man as he made his way into the half dark room. "It is only me, Mrs. Colthurst; I have come as usual to intrude upon your solitude."

"You are welcome, Captain Henry. Our doors are never shut to an old friend; but we got a start in your sudden arrival," said Mrs. Colthurst, rather coldly. "We thought it might have been my son or the Major; it is so long since they have paid us a visit."

"So you see, Guy, you must not be offended at my exclamation," said Grace, coming forward. "It would be such a novelty to see papa or Frank."

"I cannot expect my visit to be so welcome certainly, Miss Colthurst, and I must apologize for the disappointment I have given you."

" Yes, that is the best thing you can do, and in the meantime I must introduce you to my cousin Isma." If he would only transfer his affections now to her, she thought; but I could scarcely expect that, poor little Isma and I could not well be more unlike.

"Where do you come from, Captain Henry? and what news have you for us?" asked Mrs. Colthurst, as they drew round the fire again.

" Sligo has capitulated at last."

" Capitulated?" echoed Isma, with sudden interest.

" Yes. It has been long enough about it, too. No one would have ever thought that sod fort would baffle us so long."

"There were brave men behind it, I think," said Isma.

" They were obstinate at any rate; but what do you know about them, Miss O'Neil?"

" I have friends among them," said Isma, shyly. " Can you tell me where they are likely to have gone?"

" How can it concern you, Isma my dear,

to know? You are never likely to see any more of your so-called friends," said her aunt sharply.

"They will be my friends always, aunt," said Isma, colouring with vexation.

"You need not fear for them, Miss O'Neil," said Henry, who, slow though he naturally was, saw the interest his news had aroused in the young girl beside him. "The garrison of Sligo have got fair and honourable terms, and they are well on their march now to Limerick."

A grateful look was all the answer he got from Isma, who feared to trust her voice to speak further.

"And you are going in that direction, too, I suppose?" said Grace, "only with a difference: they will be inside, you outside the walls. You will be likely to change places, too, I should hope soon. How long do you give them to hold out in Limerick?"

"I can hardly say, Miss Colthurst; it is as uncertain as everything else."

"And have you really come round to my opinion, Guy, that uncertainty is the rule of life? Why, when you were here last, you propounded the doctrine of unchangeableness with great zeal. Ah! I knew you would come round to my way of thinking that it is impossible to depend on any one or anything: everything must and will change for evermore in this weary world."

"Probably you are right, Miss Colthurst, but we can hardly discuss it at present," he added in a low tone.

"Why not?" she returned; "mother has left us to our own devices, and my cousin is lost as usual in a brown study in her corner over there. What good angel brought you here to-night, Guy, just when I was fairly sick of solitude?"

"Do you really say so," he said, relaxing from the more than usual coldness of manner which he had assumed—"Do you really mean that my coming is any pleasure to you?"

"I could have welcomed any one to-night to break the stillness, and you—well, you know I might have had worse company."

"Is that all you can say, Grace, when I have come all this long way to see you, to tell you that you must be true to me—that you will break my heart, Grace, if you trifle with me?" Passionately the young man spoke, his usual reserve broken down by his strong feeling.

"Guy! why will you be so foolish? What have I done to make you care for me so much?"

"What have you done, Grace? You know what you have always been to me, how I have hung on your every word—your slightest smile; and now can you look calmly at me and ask me what you have done?"

"You are beside yourself to-night, Guy; what is the meaning of this outburst? Why cannot we go on as we have always done: we are too old friends to quarrel in this way."

"Oh, Grace! you do not know what I fear, you do not know what I should suffer were you to change to me. Tell me, Grace, only once, that no one shall ever come between you and me, and I shall never doubt you again."

"What are you thinking of, Guy? Why should any one come between our friendship? Do be reasonable; you frighten me to-night."

"Reasonable! how can I be reasonable when you talk of our friendship? And when I hear another speak of being more to you—and, Grace, it is harder to bear too, when I know how utterly unworthy he is even of your friendship."

"You have got hold of some story, I suppose, Guy; as usual you believe everything you hear. Who is the unworthy person I have been rash enough to admit to my friendship?"

"You do not know who I mean then? Perhaps after all it is untrue, but he spoke so confidently of his intimacy with you. And, Grace, Ward is not to be trusted; believe me he is——"

"Never mind what Captain Ward is in your opinion, if you please, Captain Henry, if it is to him you refer," said Grace, haughtily, while the conscious flush coloured her fair face, in spite of the usual composure which characterized her.

Guy saw the change, and turning from her, he murmured half aloud, "It is true, he has not deceived me this time after all."

"What is true, Captain Henry?" said Grace, who had caught his words.

"It is true that he is your friend—more than your friend—that you have listened to him, flirted with him, smiled at him. You cannot deny it; it is true; but you are false to me—false, Grace! and you know it."

For a moment the girl was silent; she hardly knew how to meet the passion she had excited in the usually quiet, undemonstrative man: she had encouraged him, amused herself freely with him, but still what right had he to call her to account?

"Captain Henry," she said, indignant in her turn, "you have strangely forgotten yourself to presume to call my conduct in question with any one, or the character of any one whom I may choose to make my friend."

"I have forgotten myself: you are right, Miss Colthurst, but it will be for the last time. I believed in you. I bore with you because I loved you—because I read in your smiles and your kind words that you loved me; that you were true; and I see that I have been blind, that you were deceiving me. But it is at an end now, I will never trouble you again with my presence: we part now for ever."

"Guy! you are not in earnest! - You must not leave us in this way; let us be friends as we always were."

"Friends! ah! it is too late for that now. Grace, answer me once again, have you been deceiving me all this time? Am I nothing to you?"

Steadily he looked down into those beautiful eyes, which could mock him no longer: she could not return his gaze. For a moment she felt the bitterness of the trouble she had brought upon him; and she could not find it even in her frivolous heart to deceive him again.

"No, Guy!" she said, "it is better for us

to part if we cannot be friends as we used to be."

"Better for us!" he echoed bitterly. "God only knows that! We shall never meet again in this world. Good-bye, Grace—for ever," and then he was gone.

Bewildered with the sudden turn affairs had taken, Grace sat listening to his retreating footsteps along the gallery and down the stairs, and then out into the courtyard. Gone! yes, he was surely gone, and she felt the time had passed for her to recal him. She was provoked with herself and angry with him as she thought over what had passed between them. Why had she allowed the conversation to go so far, when she saw that he was excited and more than usually demonstrative? It was foolish; they might have still been friends if she had checked him in time; but he was persistent and he had no right to take things up seriously. He might have known they could never be more than friends, why had he seized on her every word and smile and made it mean twice as much as she had ever intended?

He had presumed on their old intimacy, and tenaciously remembered the boy and girl flirtation of long ago, which ought to have been nothing to him, as it was nothing to her. And still it was a little bit of romance which was pleasant to fall back upon sometimes when there was nothing else in the way, and the sway she knew she had over him was agreeable to her vanity and love of power. Was this all at an end now? Would he keep to his determination of never seeing her again? Oh, no! that could not be ; it was only the idle threat of an angry man: he would come back, and where would be her power if their old relation to each other was not as it had been? But still, something in his look and words smote her heart, and the pain she had read in his eyes haunted her. Poor fellow! why was he such a fool? And how could she help it ? It was the old conclusion which she was just arriving at, when her cousin's voice roused her.

"Grace, Grace! what has happened? Captain Henry has left. I met him in the gallery and he would not speak; but his face— Oh! Grace, what have you done to send him away with such a look of despair?"

"What have I done, Isma? And pray what is that to you? Things have come to a pretty pass, when my conduct is called into such question," said Grace, who felt half glad to find some object to vent her irritated feelings upon.

"I could not help it, Grace, and if you had seen Captain Henry you would not wonder, but perhaps you could not help that yourself," she said, thinking of the trouble she herself so unwittingly had brought upon another.

"What do you mean, child? What do you know of such things?"

"I was in the room you know, Grace, when you and Captain Henry began talking, and I could not help seeing how he cared for you."

"Ah! you were listening, then, to our edifying conversation?" said Grace, with a scornful toss of her head.

"I did not stay to hear it; indeed I did not want to intrude upon you, Grace."

"Still you contrived to hear enough to form an opinion on the subject of Captain Henry's affections. And what about me: did I care or did I not?"

"I thought at first you did," said Isma, innocently; "but then he seemed dissatisfied, and you must have sent him away, Grace, in the end, or he would not have gone like that."

"I did not send him away, you little simpleton; he went of his own free will; and you need not look so reproachfully at me in that way."

"I did not mean to reproach you, for I suppose you could not help it, Grace: but I am so very sorry for him."

"Nonsense, child, it will do him no harm. Guy and I are always quarrelling," said Grace; "it was only a little hotter than usual to-night."

"Then it is not all over; he will come back again?"

"How can I tell, Isma? he said he would not, but that stands for nothing."

"Oh, Grace, why did you let him go? You do not know what may happen before you two may meet again."

"That is his own affair, Isma, not mine. The truth of it is he has made a fool of himself, and when I refused to do the same this is the end of it: he has no one but himself to blame." But as she said the words, she heard the echo of Guy's voice, hoarse with passion, in her ear—"False, Grace, and you know it."

CHAPTER XXXIII.

"And what remains? A useless link which cannot be undone;
A wealth of precious memories, though precious but to
one."—M.S.

THE hasty termination of Captain Henry's visit to Leagh was a very unsatisfactory proceeding to some of our other friends, who were making the most of their time in another region of the house. Will Cunningham had contrived to be of the party which was accompanying Captain Henry to the scene of war near Limerick. And Winny, who, since the memorable ride from Sligo, had ceased to look upon him as her especial enemy to be bantered and brow-beaten on all possible occasions, welcomed him almost with cordiality.

"So you've turned up again, Master Will, and good luck to you; but it's a godsend to see a face a body knows now-a-days. And how goes the world with you since you rode this way afore?"

"Tolerable well, thank you, Mistress Winny; the times is hard, and the day's march long and heavy to get over, even for a man that's a soldier born and bred, like your humble servant. But they tell me the fighting's nigh hand over, and sure it seems likely that the spirit is dying out of the country when it comes that you're pleasured to see the sight of an enemy's face, Mistress Winny," said Will, with a comical look on his own visage.

"Pleasured indeed, young man! But you're mighty sharp in your observations; and just take my advice, and don't count your chickens before they're hatched. There's a deal more spirit in the country than the likes o' you knows of, and you don't know the turn it may take yet; so be easy and cautious-like in your speech, young man."

"To be sure, Winny, there's nothing like caution, as your old crook-backed master, Sir Teague himself, has observed in my hearing before now: and there's spirit enough in some of the fellows, God knows! when they go a-galloping and a-rampaging through the country like some of your friends, Winny, that we met on the road from Sligo. Perhaps you're a-wishing for a ride with the likes of him?"

"Nonsense, Will. It's that sort that takes the right spirit out of the decent folk in the country: but you know yourself you've some hard riders among yourselves that are as lawless as our own Rapparees."

"You're right, truly, in that quarter, mistress, and I've had as hard a ride with our young Captain, who is here to-day, after some of our own Militia fellows, as ever Galloping Will rode himself."

"Then there's no reason for you to boast yourselves a bit better than ourselves, Mr. Drummer. There's faults on both sides by your own showing: so we're pretty well quits."

"I've no manner of objection to the bargain, mistress; and it's just possible that out of the wrongs of both sides we may hit it off right between us. What do you say to that, Winny?"

"That depends, young man, on what meaning you put upon the right."

"Come now, Winny, you know well enough what I mean. We hit it off pretty right, I reckon, when we found it such easy travelling together on our road here—righter, I humbly presume, than if you'd a-gone off with that galloping thief who had such an uncommon fancy for your pretty face. Eh, Winny, what do you say to that?"

"You done me a service, Master Will, sure enough, that blessed day, and I'm pretty well bound to keep a civil tongue in my head to ye: but be easy, man, and don't push things too far all of a sudden like."

"As you will, Winny, my good girl. We'll do the thing gradual if it pleases you. But how now? Surely that's the Captain's voice in the court-yard. What the devil can he mean by moving on at this hour? Bedad, he couldn't have been as comfortable as you or I, Winny."

Very stern and dark was Guy Henry's countenance as he turned his horse's head hastily from Leagh. The night was wild, and the heavy banks of clouds looked darker and more lowering when from time to time a gleaming flood of moonlight shone out from behind them. Once more he looked back, before the tall trees, waving and moaning in the storm, hid the grey walls of the house from his sight. How changed was the scene from that last time, when in the early summer morning he had ridden away and turned to look back as he did now! Then the sun shone out over the trees, their branches gently stirred by the morning breeze and gilded in the glowing light which bathed the whole picture, glancing round the fair head which bent forward to see the last of the little party, adding warmth to the smile which seemed to follow him, and deepening the colour of the rose which he carried away. Where were all those charms now? The sunshine seemed gone for ever, and only the cold fitful moonbeams were left in its place to cast the long shadows of the restless trees across the turret-window, all closed and darkened now. Never more would that fair, smiling face watch him as he rode away. She would watch for another, perhaps, to come and go, and the roses would blossom and bask in the warm sunlight, and another would carry them away and know their sweetness; but for him—Guy Henry—there would be no more smiles, no more roses. Even the moon hid herself as he glanced back once more, and nothing but the black masses of heavy rain-clouds were to be seen over the dark trees. He knew now that he had lived only for those smiles and those roses, and they had been given to him falsely, carelessly, meaning nothing. He had been the dupe of a pretty, heartless girl, who had given him her empty smiles and fading roses, while he had given her his whole heart; and to her it was as nothing. It mattered not what his fate was now : he would court the danger the ever-present thought of her had led him to avoid in past days; he would seek in the foremost ranks for rest from a life from which the sun had gone out for ever.

CHAPTER XXXIV.

> "Dispute it like a man.
>   I shall do so;
> But I must also feel it as a man:
> I cannot but remember such things were,
> That were most precious."—SHAKSPEARE.

"HAVE you no volunteer work? no active duty you can send me on, sir?" said a young man with a grave, anxious face to his Colonel, as they talked together in the camp of the English army lying around the closely-besieged town of Limerick.

"Why, Henry, have you not had enough of the wild life yet?"

"No, Colonel Mitchelburne," said Guy Henry, for it was he. "I cannot rest here: this comparatively inactive life does not suit me. Surely there is some stirring work to be done about the country?"

"Yes, I have no doubt there is plenty still. The Rapparees are pretty active, in spite of all our efforts to put them down: but why, Henry, is this restless fit? You are generally content enough to follow the fortunes of the regiment."

A flush came over the young man's face, and he hesitated before he answered in a husky voice—

"I have always felt that I have been in the right place, sir, when I was with you; but now it is different. I am changed, I think."

"Perhaps it is I who have changed, Henry? Have you any reason for dissatisfaction?"

"No, sir," he said calmly, steadying his voice with an effort. "It is I who have changed. I have become restless, as you say, and want excitement to work the fit off. You will oblige me, Colonel, if you can arrange any expedition I could be of use in."

"It is an easy enough matter these days. Some few of us, perhaps, would willingly confess to have had more change and excitement than they care for. But, Henry, I fear you have some reason for this restlessness. What is it? Can I lend you a helping hand only by sending you away to run into danger, perhaps to meet death?"

Kindly the Colonel looked at his young officer, and saw the deep lines of trouble on his face.

"You can do nothing else for me, sir. I have been unfortunate: only let me do something, and perhaps the rest may come."

"There is rest to be found in work sometimes, Henry: you are right in that, certainly. I will see what can be done."

"Thank you, sir."

Guy turned away: his thoughts of rest still lay beyond the daily round of work the Colonel had spoken of.

It was no difficult matter to make out dangerous and exciting work in those days: the disturbed state of the country, and the numerous bands of Rapparees roaming about in all directions, continually called for active measures. Colonel Mitchelburne was not much at a loss to find an opportunity of complying with Captain Henry's request. A Rapparee captain whom we have heard something of before, and well known in the country as "Galloping Hogan," had, with a party of eighty men, surprised and taken Camgart Castle, about six miles from the town of Birr. To drive them from this stronghold before they saw fit to burn it down, which was the general fate of all buildings falling into the hands of those lawless bands, was the object of the expedition Captain Henry's company was soon detached for.

"What is the meaning of this, Henry?" said his old friend Frank Colthurst, as he confronted him, hurrying to carry out the orders for the march. They had met but seldom lately, although in the same camp, for Guy had been in no humour to seek out the company of any who were associated in his mind with the dark cloud that had fallen upon him. Turning coldly from Colthurst now, he answered shortly—

"What do you allude to?"

"This sudden fancy you have taken for

foraging expeditions. You were ever wont to leave such duty to more enterprising fellows. Mitchelburne tells me it is volunteer service on your part."

"He is right; I asked him to make out something of the sort for me. But you mistake. It is not exactly a foraging expedition: there is real work to be done, I believe."

"Ay, a castle or something of the sort to be seen after—exciting, I dare say, but hazardous too, I suspect. Those Rapparee fellows are cunning dogs enough; they are well up to this sort of work. Take care of yourself at any rate, Guy. We can't afford to lose so steady a man."

"My loss would scarcely matter to any one, I am rather inclined to think," said Guy, his brow contracting.

"How now, old fellow! you are in the blues. What has come over you lately? You have not shown as usual. You used to track my footsteps like a pet dog, Guy, and many a kick or a cuff I dare say you got; but you didn't seem to mind in those days. I used to say you had the thickest hide of any poor devil I ever met. What's the change, man?"

"The thickest skin will wear out some time, Frank, I suppose," said Guy, moodily.

"Ay, is that the case? Have I worn out even your patience with my impudence? But you have not come under my thraldom much lately; it can't be my doing. What has Grace been up to. That's the question more likely."

Careless though his words were, Frank looked keenly and anxiously at his companion, whom in his easy-going way he had always liked, and even respected, though so different in every possible particular from himself. Quietly Guy returned the glance, and answered calmly—

"Yes, the story is easily guessed : your sister took the trouble to make a fool of me, and she succeeded. For the future it is as well for us—for me at least—to avoid all reference to the past: you have had no part in this affair, but for the present I would rather not even see you. My time is short now. I must be off."

"Stay a moment, Guy. I am sorry for you;" and Frank clasped his hand warmly, forgetting the usual cold worldly wisdom which was generally the uppermost consideration in his mind. "You knew Grace, Guy; you knew what she was, why did you let her deceive you in this way?"

"Yes, I knew how merry and light-hearted she was, and I was a fool to think she could ever care for me. It is all over and done now, Frank: we shall never meet again, only before I go I would warn you, her brother, that she will be deceived in her turn."

"What do you mean, Guy? Has she anything else on hand now?"

"You will, perhaps, think it is not fair of me to prejudice you against another; but, Frank, though the past can never be undone for me, and sometimes I feel that even if I could I would not alter it, for I see now how impossible—how improbable it was that she and I could have made each other happy, still I would that she were happy, and I tell you, Frank, Ward is not worthy of her, nor is he what she thinks him to be. If he marries her, it is only carrying out his old game of speculation. This is no jealous fancy, believe me; it is only but too real. There is no need for me to say more, she may find it out for herself: but, at any rate, I have warned you, and I could do nothing else."

"This is some nonsense you have got into your head, Henry. Ward, what has he to do with it? Why, man, he cannot have been more than once at Leagh: and surely Grace would hardly imagine he was much of a spec. He can't be; it is absurd. But good-bye now, old fellow, if you must be off: forget all about Grace and her speculations. You would not have suited each other, as you say yourself : get over it, man, and mind you come back all right, and we shall have as merry days as ever yet at Leagh. If you only knew how many little affairs of this sort I have lived out, it would give you courage."

"Yes, I daresay," said Guy, with a grave, sad look in his eyes. "I am a coward, but perhaps it will not be so always. Good-bye, Frank; we are friends to the last, and tell her that I shall never trouble her with my stupidity again. She made some days very bright for me, and the darkness will soon pass away."

Not many minutes later, he was in his saddle, leading his little troop towards Camgart Castle.

CHAPTER XXXV.

"Sudden and swift a whistling ball
Came out of the wood, and the voice was still."
—LONGFELLOW.

THE country was desolate and deserted through which they rode, the harvest in many places left ungathered, trodden down, and destroyed by the wind and rain, while blackened ruins of hamlets here and there bespoke the recent presence of those wild, lawless spirits of whom they were in pursuit.

Steadily they went on their way to Carolante, where the Earl of Drogheda's regiment was in garrison. Although within about a mile from Camgart, a very imperfect account could be obtained here of the enemy's doings, and Captain Henry and his party, uncertain whether the castle was actually in the hands of the rebels, as they had been led to believe, or not, proceeded cautiously towards it. Neither enemy nor friend was to be seen; an almost death-like stillness hung over the country, while before them rose the dark battlements of the castle: standing on a slightly rising ground, its weather-beaten turrets seemed to touch the heavy lowering clouds which darkened the horizon. No sound was to be heard, except the low twittering of the birds as they wheeled and fluttered over-head, in expectation of a storm from the gathering clouds. No appearance of life or motion was to be seen on the castle walls, and even a thin curl of smoke, from a cabin half hidden in the trees, scarcely rose beyond the low roof in the heavy atmosphere.

Perplexed and uncertain what course to pursue, Henry gave the word to halt as they drew near the shelter of a thickly planted orchard. There he posted his little company, not more than a musket shot from the castle, and followed by Will Cunningham, who was of the party, and another man, he stole on towards the castle, which, from its quiet appearance, he felt almost sure had been deserted. The castle gate was nearly reached, and still no sound of life was heard, earth-works freshly thrown up seemed deserted, and no one was to be seen except a solitary woman slowly moving in the direction of the cabin, her slight figure bending under the weight of a pitcher of water. Unknown to Henry and his companions, she had watched them as they approached, and gathering from their dress and green badges that they were English soldiers, her first thought was that they were in danger. Did she not know that behind those seemingly deserted earth-heaps a score of bayonets were fixed for death— certain death for all who advanced with those hostile colours? Her sympathies were certainly for those behind the ramparts, their leader was more to her than her own life: none knew so well as she his unrelenting, bloodthirsty spirit, but, with a woman's pity for the weaker side in her heart, she shuddered to see the three men, young and full of life as they were, quietly drawing nearer step by step to certain ruin. With a hasty impulse she raised her hand to sign to them that the enemy were near, and, but imperfectly understanding her meaning, Henry hesitated and stopped. Every movement had been watched by those in the castle, and his sudden stop seemed as a signal for action. In an instant the silence of the evening was broken by a volley; loud and resounding it echoed from the turreted walls, frightening the birds in their restless flights, and startling the woman in her shelter among the trees, her pitcher falling in a thousand pieces by her side, while heavy drops fell quickly from the leaden clouds over-head.

Slowly the smoke cleared away, but the three figures stealthily advancing are not there; the volley has done its work well, only one figure moves now, bending with a frightened, terror-stricken face over his fallen comrades. Never more now could Grace Colthurst's dazzling smiles fascinate or wound Guy Henry's heart. His rest had come, and the darkness was past for him. With trembling hands, Will Cunningham felt for any sign of life; all was over with the prostrate forms beside him, and quick-witted as he was by nature, he lay quietly by their side, lest the enemy should think it necessary to repeat the volley. The quickly gathering darkness closed around, and he crawled back through the now heavily falling rain to the shelter of the orchard, where his companions cowered, frightened and perplexed.

"The Captain?" was the anxious question as he drew near.

" Laid low, and Morton too," was the short answer.

"Mercy on us, but it was quick work, the ruffians! They've never done for a better gentleman or a stouter-hearted soldier than yonder poor fellow, and what's to become of us now; lads, we're not safe here to wait for daylight?" said one of the men.

"The Captain's body must be got, no matter who's in danger, I tell ye," said Will, stoutly. "Who'll follow me to the rescue?"

" And come in for another volley like the last, Will? Why, man, have you not had enough of the fellows' powder and shot yet?" said the same speaker.

" It's too dark, man, to find them," said another.

" You're right, lads, " said one who had not spoken before, and seemed to raise his voice in authority. " I'd give a good deal the Captain had come scot-free of this adventure, but the deed's done now: we must see to our own safety, and watch for the first glimpse of dawn to guide us to our friends at Carolante."

CHAPTER XXXVI.

*"Peace; come away: the song of woe
Is after all an earthly song."—*TENNYSON.

THE next morning the little troop found their way back to Carolante, with saddened faces and heavy hearts. Their Captain and one of their comrades who had only a few hours before ridden the same road with them, both so full of life and activity, would never more be among their number. The Captain's kindly voice was silent now, the brave heart would never beat for joy or sorrow again, nor the steady hand guide the rein of the horse now led mournfully along with his saddle empty.

A Drum was ordered by the officer in command at Carolante to return without delay to claim the fallen officer's body, that the last honours might be paid to it by his friends. Will Cunningham was told off for this sad mission; and as he drew near the place where they had stood—

he and those two others who had been taken while he was left—he looked eagerly for any trace of their remains. Clearly enough he could discern the exact spot where they had halted on the signal from the woman, and he could almost have believed no time had elapsed since he had turned to that familiar face by his side to see what course should be pursued, when the sudden change came and the clouds of smoke enveloped them in an instant. There was the castle before him, still looking dark and sombre, though this time the sun was shining. The heavy rain-clouds had spent themselves, and once more the blue sky appeared and the thin wreath of smoke, from the cabin among the trees, curled and twined upwards in the lightened atmosphere. Again the woman's figure was to be seen not far off: but to-day she bore no pitcher; in a thousand pieces it lay half buried in the tangled grass. Making his way over to where she stood watching him, with curious eyes, he asked her curtly why she did not signal for a volley to do its work on him.

"I meant to save you if it were possible, not to do you harm," she answered in a suppressed voice; "God knows no other thought was in my mind when I raised my hand last evening."

"That's all very fine, my good girl, but you don't expect me to believe that you are not in league with yonder devils, who fired like cowards from their ditches, and did for our poor Captain, God bless him!"

"The Lord knows, my heart had pity for you when I saw you on your way unknownst of the danger; and when the guns flashed from the castle, and your comrades fell, I sorrowed for them, I tell you, as if I had been their friend."

"Much good that could do them, you fool!" said Will, gruffly. "But come now, tell me what they have done with them, that's more to the purpose than all your woman's chatter?"

"I saw them at the first glimpse of dawn steal out and carry in the bodies, if that's what you mean, sir. Poor fellows!

but my heart bled for them as I thought of the woman-kind who would miss them in the days to come."

"Ah! you know likely what such a thing is, girl?" said Will, less roughly, as he looked with more interest on the pale face of the girl before him. Very young she seemed, though her dark grey eyes were shaded with a care-worn, saddened look, that told of suffering unusual for one of her years.

"Ay! I know what it is to miss and to hunger for a face; the Lord himself knows that's what I do."

"What brings you here, girl? This is not your home, I'll be bound," said Will.

"Neither it is. I've no home, no place waiting for me: but I will have—yes, he has promised it, and I will follow him, on and on, and wait and wait, till the time comes, and he will make his promises good." Passionately she spoke, wringing her hands with a half wild expression in her beautiful eyes.

"Who is it, girl? Who has had the heart

to leave you?" said Will, compassionate in his turn.

"Who? And what is that to you? Go your own ways, man, and let me and him alone. Coward did you call him just now? He's no coward! There's not his like in all Ireland, that there's not! and I know him better than any one in this wide world."

"But why are you not with him? Why are you this side you castle walls?"

"He does not know I am here," she said, more calmly. "I follow him everywhere he goes, and I swore I would follow him to the end: there's no one has a better right; he is mine—mine altogether."

"But why not wait till he is ready for you, till the war-time is over."

"I cannot rest without him; he made me love him, and now it can't be undone. I must be near him, or they will kill him. I know they want to kill him. You want to kill him," she said almost fiercely; "but I tell ye it's harder than you think to catch Galloping Hogan. Catch him! Catch him if you can!" and she laughed derisively. Will turned away, his heart sad for the poor girl, half mad in her love for the wild daring ruffian who had left her, as he had perhaps many another, without one regretful thought: and Winny, who was a constant image in Drummer Will's imagination lately, had run the risk of a like fate.

Cautiously approaching the castle, Will beat a parley, and gained an interview with its Captain. Hogan was a powerfully-built, handsome man, his wild life showing itself in the dark bronze colour of his face, and the grizzled, untrimmed beard and hair which gave him an almost savage appearance. Keenly he eyed our friend the drummer, who needed all his natural assurance to confront the lion in his den.

" We have met before, av' I mistake not?" said Hogan.

"It is not unlikely, Captain. We're neither of us likely to bide much beside the hearthstone, so we may pretty well calculate on knocking hardly again' each other now and then."

"Ay, man! But have you no recollection of a summer's evening not so long ago, and a scrimmage, and bloody heads, and a girl into the bargain? Eh! I've hit the mark, I see, my man," he said with a mocking laugh as he noticed the angry colour mount up on Will's face. "Never mind, man, you thought you outdone me, did you? but there are girls enough and to spare for you and me, so we need not quarrel on that score. What's your business with me to-day? Speak, fellow, and get you gone. I'd sooner have something better to look at than you, do you understand?"

"My errand is soon told, Captain, and by my father's faith I'll not peril my soul within your cursed walls an instant past my time. I have come from my commanding officer at Carolante, to demand the bodies of our gallant Captain and his comrade who fell before your walls yesterday."

"Ay, they were brave fellows to venture so close, no doubt: but all the same it's a foolish game, and I reckon you've got a lesson not to follow in their steps, honest man. And now you want the poor devils' bodies to say your foolish prayers and make your preaching over; but I'll tell you you're mistaken if you think I'm going to treat with you as in a fair fight. You treat us when you catch us as you please, and it's my notion turn about is fair play, so you may take yourself back, Mr. Drummer, and tell them as sent you that rogues, as they call us Rapparees, stand by their own laws. The gentleman that has fallen will be honourably dealt with by me, for I have come across him too before, and I know him to have had a brave heart, so he will be decently put under ground, as becomes the like of him. And now you've got your answer, Mr. Drummer, and these are hot quarters for those who have got the word to be off."

"It's not for me to say agin you, Captain," said Will, resolutely standing his ground. "The law's in your own hands here, it is true, but for the sake of him who will never hold a musket before you again, speak the word that his own Drum may beat the march before him to the grave. He was a brave and a true gentleman, as you said yourself, and as you'd have known better too, if you had seen him as I have seen him, up and down the country this time past."

" As you will, man, though it's not much satisfaction it will give the poor fellow now as to who beats the drum or lets it alone. But a soger must have his due anyhow, so see that the thing is done properly av' you will, man."

Under the shadow of the castle walls the lonely graves were dug, and as the last rays of the autumn sun were lighting up the yellowing leaves of the trees around, and shedding a warm glow on the freshly turned sod, the bodies of the two soldiers were borne from the castle to the deep roll of the drum, which so often before had roused them to action and cheered them on through many a weary march. This was all over for them now, never more would the tired feet struggle on along the dusty wayside, or the home-sick heart beat with excitement for the sound of coming footsteps to meet them in deadly feud. The drum had beat its last note for them, the sun shone down for the last time on their pathway, and glistened on the green grass which was replaced once more in that quiet corner under the castle walls. Three times the sharp sound of a volley rang through the still evening air, and then the little group dispersed. The nightfall came again, the shadows deepening over the old castle and the thick trees, but darkness and sorrow would come no more to cast their shadow over Guy Henry: the light had dawned for him at last.

CHAPTER XXXVII.

> "The bold they kill, th' unwary they surprise,
> Who fights finds death, and death finds him who flies
> The warders of the gate; but scarce maintain
> Th' unequal combat and resist in vain."—POPE.

THE end of September was near, and affairs in Limerick seemed to be coming to a crisis. Provisions were beginning to be scarce, and all hope of relief from France was set aside by the knowledge that the mouth of the Shannon was guarded by English men-of-war. The aspect of the city was sadly changed since we were last within its walls; then all was bustle and excitement, the garrison preparing hopefully for the struggle, in which they had been conquerors only one short year ago. Now a weary listlessness has crept over the people, hope has well nigh died out of the bravest hearts: their walls are shattered and dismantled, their houses in some places blackened ruins, ammunition is nearly exhausted, and each day seems to bring the enemy nearer and nearer to their homes. It was the evening of the day when the enemy, having crossed the river, had attacked the fort which protected the Thomond Bridge. The struggle was over: of eight hundred men who garrisoned the fort only a hundred and twenty escaped into the town. The drawbridge leading to the city had been drawn up by order of the officer in command of the Irish, to keep the besiegers from following the fugitives; many of the Irish perished in the river, and the rest fell victims to the unrestrained fury of their enemies. Wearied with anxiety and excitement, Sarsfield's wife and niece sat listening for tidings of the encounter. The last weeks had passed heavily for them as well as for the other inmates of the town. Disappointment and trouble had left their traces on their worn faces, pale with the privations and imprisonment they had endured. The old servant, Margaret, more bowed and withered looking than ever, droned her mournful ditty in a corner of the room, while the General's little son, the only light-hearted one of the party, amused himself at her side.

Suddenly the old woman started up from her low seat near the window.

"They are coming, my lady, they are coming! I hear the tramp of the horse, and they come too fast for victory. Holy Mother of God, they fly! Our brave lads are driven back to the walls by the tyrants."

Eagerly the two ladies pressed towards the window which overlooked the street, and too surely were the old woman's words verified. In wild terror and confusion the troops were hurrying back from the disastrous scene of action. Furious with the sights they had seen of their comrades hurled, by the drawing up of the bridge, into the river, or left to the mercy of the English, the multitude clamoured for revenge on the officer who had issued the order but who had, happily for himself, fallen mortally wounded in the act of shutting the Thomond Gate. Cries for capitulation were heard on all sides, and it seemed as if the crisis of the struggle had come at last.

"Thank God, he is safe! Aunt, look, he comes this way," said Mary Sarsfield, drawing her aunt's attention to a group of officers who seemed vainly endeavouring to calm the people. Patrick Sarsfield, now Earl of Lucan, was in their midst, his tall figure distinguishable above the others. The sudden death of Tyrconnell some weeks previously had placed the command nominally in the hands of the Lords Justices, but in reality Sarsfield and D'Usson held the reins. The latter, wearied with the struggle which detained him in a foreign land, would gladly lay down his arms, and even Sarsfield's energy began to fail as he saw each day the inevitable catastrophe drawing nearer.

"We have been driven back—beaten," he said, bitterly, in answer to the unspoken questions on his wife's face, when he joined them after dispersing the mob in the streets.

"The horse gave in; but what else

could they do, undisciplined recruits as they were?"

"Is all lost?" said his wife, in a suppressed voice of despair, while her niece could not restrain the bitter tears which fell fast as she watched her uncle's face, which told her all hope of ultimate deliverance was extinguished.

"I fear so," he said, despondingly. "The people have lost all patience; they will not hold out any longer. We must submit. Scott, is that you?" he said, as a tall figure appeared in the doorway and our old friend Colonel Scott advanced.

"Yes, General, I followed you in," said he, courteously saluting the ladies. "The last blow is struck, I fear. What is to be done?"

"D'Usson, have you seen him?"

"Yes, he is completely dumb-foundered, and declares the spirit of the people will never rise after this day's work."

"Ay, he has only been waiting for this opportunity to speak: he has long known the end was inevitable."

"And you, Colonel Scott, have you no hope, no prospect of success for us?" asked Mary.

"I have seen sufficient the last few hours, Miss Sarsfield, to break down any hope I had, and I must confess I have not had much to boast of for some time past."

"Why will you all be so faint-hearded?" she said, impetuously. "Uncle, you are strong still, you will not let them give in. Remember this is our last chance!" and she bent over her uncle's chair and looked into his face for the energy which till now had never failed.

"Mary, you do not know how it is," he said, sadly. "Could you have seen our poor fellows to-day, cut down ruthlessly, unable almost to strike a blow—had you heard the wretched people, maddened by the sight, and weak and wretched in their want and suffering, you would know too well there is nothing for it but to yield."

"To yield!" she echoed. "Must this be the end of it all?"

"Better now than later, Miss Sarsfield,"

said Colonel Scott, interested in the girl's passionate sorrow.

"Why do you say that? Do you want to gain their favour too by submission? Is there anything worth living for, that we should sell ourselves to gain? Colonel Scott, do you care for life so much that you will not risk it any longer in the struggle?"

"Life has not much to offer for me, Miss Sarsfield, but you are young: have you no thought for yourself, no hope in the future in another land?"

"All my hopes are here," she said, "in Ireland, a free independent Ireland, and now it will be so different! What is France to me? I care not to live there."

"Mary, child, you are taking it too much to heart," said her uncle, tenderly caressing her hand as it lay on his chair. "You are young, as Colonel Scott says, and there will be brighter prospects far, for you in France, than you ever could have here. Why, child, you do not know how the sun shines there, and, please God, it will shine on you as cheerily as on any."

"France is nothing to me. I care not how bright it may be there; it will be dark here in our own Ireland; the people will be oppressed and persecuted if we forsake them now. If we give in now we can never help them again. But every one betrays them: it is all the same, no one will have patience to the end."

"Miss Sarsfield, you are too hard on us. You forget that our interests are in common with the people; that if we betray them, as you call it, we betray ourselves. You surely would not urge us to risk again such numbers of lives as we have lost by to-day's disaster?"

"I have spoken too strongly, perhaps, but you do not know how I love our country, and how terrible the thought is to me of leaving her to the English, who have no pity, no mercy for us."

"Perhaps they will after all have more mercy for us than some of our own people. Had we been all true to ourselves this day would never have come."

"You are too truly right, Scott," said

the Earl, his keen eyes flashing with indignation. "Those who have promised the most have failed us soonest. Why, it is but a few short weeks ago when in this very room we talked with the Baldearg, and even Mary there could not have been more enthusiastic than he was in the cause. And now where is he, and all the power and patriotism he boasted so loudly of?"

A deep flush rose in the young girl's cheek at the mention of that name. No one had built so much as she had done on this man's faith. How she had listened here in this very spot to his eloquent words! She heard the echo of them now ringing in her ears, in that soft rich tone which had stamped itself upon her memory. She saw the tall graceful form and the full dark eyes of her hero as he had looked down into hers, and she had felt that in him all her dreams might be realized: and now where was he, and where were all his brave words and daring looks? What had they done for Ireland or the Irish, what had been their value? Only just as much as the chaff blown hither and thither at the mercy of the wind. Full of these thoughts she heard no more of the conversation around her, as they discussed the ways and means which must be taken to save their town and their countrymen from starvation and death by the offer of terms to the enemy.

CHAPTER XXXVIII.

*" His promises were, as he then was mighty;
But his performance, as he is now, nothing."*
                                                    SHAKSPEARE.

"Miss Mary, acushla! don't ye take on so, now don't ye!" said old Margery, as she drew near her young mistress, who, thinking herself alone, had buried her head in her hands in a bitter fit of unrepressed sorrow.

"Only wait, alanna, and all will come right, never you fear! Did I not hear the General, your own uncle, my blessing, say just a while past, 'Who knows but a bright day may dawn for us yet over the water? We'll come back, maybe, with fresh strength and teach them a different lesson.' So dry your eyes, acushla, and leave the sorrowing to them who has brought it on themselves; it's not for the like o' you to be dimming your young eyes before their time, mavourneen."

"Oh, Margery, Margery, there is no hope now! Nothing to look forward to! No one to trust!"

"Ahone, ahone! Miss Mary, acushla, but you're over young to sing that song. Look at me, and tell me, if it plaze you, there's no hope, no nothing for me; but, blessings on you, my beauty, you'll live to see many a hope and a sorrow live and die itself out all natural-like and aisy."

"I did not think you would have cared so little, Margery, but you are like all the rest. Even Ireland is nothing to you when it comes to living or dying."

"Blessings on ye, acushla, there's nobody takes that kindly to the dying, more by token, mavourneen, when not a ha'porth's to be got by it! Why even yonder brave gentleman that was a talking a while back to ye—though I heard him say, and there was sorrow in his eye too as he said it, ' he had'nt over much to live for '—bedad, Miss Mary, even the likes o' him would look over his shoulder and take a second thought before he sat down to wait for his pulse to stop its beating and the cold sweat of death to steal gradual-like over him."

"And what is there to live for, Mar? It seems as if there was nothing or nobody to trust in again."

"Take courage, acushla! The Lord will look to his own, and send help to our own green isle in good time."

"You have told me so before, Margery, many and many a time, but no good has ever come. Did you not tell me Baldearg would help us, that he would deliver us from our enemies, and what has he done? He has come and gone, and we are worse off than before. No, Margery, it is no use trying to make me trust in any one again: there must be a curse over us, nothing turns to good for us here."

"Whisht, whisht, Miss Mary! It's an ill thing to speak such words, and it's not for the likes o' us poor weak women to understand the doings of such as the Baldearg, God bless him!"

"You don't mean to say, Margery, that you have faith still in him?"

"Bedad, and it's not for me to doubt the likes o' the Baldearg. Come what may, sure he's himself and no mistake, acushla!"

"But why has he deserted us? Why did he speak such fair words and put such hope into our hearts?"

"The Lord only knows, Miss, honey, what's in the heart of any one, let alone a man like the Baldearg, who comes and goes like the wandering light of the fairies on a bog side. But depend upon it, Miss, jewel, the Baldearg knows what he's about and no mistake, the Lord bless him and save him!"

"He knows how to take care of himself at any rate, Margery," said the Lady Honora, who, returning to the room, had heard the old woman's last remark. "But, Mary, my dear, we must recognise the will of a higher power in this matter, and take even the hardest fate from His hands without this questioning."

"Yes, I know it, Aunt. I am wrong to give way in this manner: but you do not know all I have thought and dreamt about it, and now everything I believed in seems false."

" I think I can understand your feelings, Mary dear, we have all been deceived more or less by fair words and promises; but there is good yet to be sought and found if we have patience."

" Patience, Aunt! What do you mean? Patience will not bring us back the faith that is lost."

" No, dear, but it may teach us where to look for true faith, which will not fail us in the end."

" I will never have faith in any one again I think, Aunt. He seemed so true, so earnest in the cause."

" He did, dear, and others were deceived as well as you: besides, we do not know all his motives, all his temptations."

" We know enough, Aunt, and, no matter where we go and what happens, I hope we shall never see him again."

" You are right, Mary, it would be better not, and you are too true yourself to waste your faith on what is false. There is much to be done and thought about now; we need all our energies to work for others."

"Yes, we must not spend any more time over these fancies. I have been a fool, but it is over now: we must never speak again about this, Aunt."

"No, dear, we need all to be brave now and must forget our own selfish cares. Listen! Is that not your uncle's voice? Come, dear, he needs all the help we can give him more than ever; no one knows the disappointment this failure has been to him."

The following evening, the day after the fight at the Thomond Gate, after anxious consultations within the city, the town drums beat a parley, and an interview was arranged between Sarsfield and the Marquis de Ruvigny. Long and earnestly the two brave men spoke together. They could understand each other without prejudice, for both were actuated by a single-hearted desire for the welfare of the cause each sustained. The Marquis for his part knew what it was to give up his country and his people for religious principles, principles which, though entirely opposed to those of the man at his side, still taught him to reverence with charity the scruples of another equally sincere and well-meaning as himself. He listened therefore with courtesy to the stipulations of the patriotic Irishman for the toleration of his religion and the freedom of his country. An armistice was the immediate result of this conference, and negotiations were entered upon to bring the siege to a close without further loss of time. It is not in the province of this tale to touch on the merits or demerits of the treaty which, after a couple of days, was agreed upon, and awaited only the arrival of the Lords Justices for its completion. In the meantime all hostilities were suspended, prisoners were set at liberty, and the two armies met on equal terms within and without the city.

CHAPTER XXXIX.

"Forgiveness may be spoken with the tongue,
Forgiveness may be written with the pen,
But think not that the parchment and mouth pardon
Will e'er eject old hatreds from the heart."—TAYLOR.

IT was the third of October, and many of the Irish officers were assembled at dinner in the tent of the Duke of Wirtemburg. A stranger would hardly have guessed that these men, now so perfectly harmonious round the social board, had so lately been the bitterest of sworn enemies. Jokes circulated, stories were told of the experiences of the campaign, the light-hearted French and Irish natures provoking the stolid English and Dutch to forget for a time their habitual reserve. Animated as most of the faces were round the table, there were saddened hearts among them: the struggle and the hardships were over, it was true, but there was a blank sense of failure and loss in the thoughts of our Irish friends which they could not escape from. The future lay before them hazy and uncertain: their ties were broken, their prospects changed and clouded; a fresh start must be made, a new life begun, and how and where was it to be? such questions filled many a brave heart with gloomy, restless forebodings. Sarsfield especially allowed these thoughts to weigh upon him, and even as he talked and laughed with those around him, as it was his genial nature to do, a closer observer might have detected the shadows of disquietude on his anxious face. As far as he himself was concerned, there was no hesitation as to what course he should pursue. France was of course his destination for the present; but in the future his plans and schemes would fail, could he not influence a considerable number of his countrymen to follow his example. Full permission to go or stay as they chose, had been secured for the people by the articles of treaty, but the Irish for the most part were disinclined to leave their native land, even in the prospect of a triumphant return, which Sarsfield and his friends built their hopes upon.

"Is your determination to leave the country still unchanged, Lord Lucan," asked an English officer who sat near him.

"Could you conceive it possible, Major Colthurst, for me to take any other course?" returned the Earl, quickly.

"To tell you the truth, General, I cannot understand your motive in banishing yourself willingly from a country you profess to love, and where you may have every prospect of a quiet life, which I would think desirable after the campaign you have come through."

"A quiet life did you say, Major? I am afraid such will never fall to my lot: besides, there are one or two obstacles in the way of my contenting myself in this country as it will be in the future."

"To be sure it is not quite as you would wish, General, but why not accept the inevitable and let bygones be bygones. You have done your best to fight against fate, and now you owe it to your country to stick by her, and give your energies to her aid. For my part I have had quite enough of this campaigning: it is sadly unprofitable work at the best of times."

"Some of your people cannot have that story to tell, I should say, sir," observed Colonel Scott, who had no scruple in interrupting a conversation which he knew could scarcely be congenial to his General.

"What reason have you for such an inference, may I ask, Colonel Scott?" said the Major, stiffly.

"I have been unfortunate enough to see rather too much of what we call preying in our part of the country not to know that some one must have profited considerably by the common loss, Major Colthurst."

"Ay, ay, I suppose so," said the Major, innocently. "Good cattle in your parts, eh? A temptation, certainly, to see stray herds about the country when one's bawn is provokingly empty."

"You come from the north, I think, Colonel?" asked Frank Colthurst, who was not far off. "I have heard strange stories from one of our militia fellows of the doings down there. One Ward—Lindesay Ward —did you happen to hear of him?"

"One of Mitchelburne's refractory fellows, I think," answered the Colonel. "He will know more about him than I do."

"That is the young fellow you introduced some time ago to me, I think, Frank?" said his father. "A fine young fellow, too, with not a bad idea of the value of stock. Ay! I remember him; he spoke of being at Leagh, too. What do you want to know about him, Frank?"

"I merely asked Colonel Scott if he knew him, sir. I believe it was somehow through poor Henry he got to Leagh."

"Ah! poor Guy! He was an old friend of yours, Frank."

"He was, sir; and I could wish now that he had never seen us or Leagh."

They had risen from the table, and father and son stood together somewhat apart from the others.

"Why, Frank, what harm did the poor fellow ever do to any of us?"

"The harm was to himself, sir, not to us. We all know pretty well how to take care of ourselves, I think; but poor Henry made a mess of it; or rather Grace did it for him."

"Grace! Nonsense, Frank: what had the poor girl to say to his misfortunes?" The Major spoke almost harshly, for Grace was his favourite child.

Frank, more quick-witted and calculating by nature, was liable at times to perceive and see through the petty foibles of his father in a way which was by no means comfortable or pleasant; while Grace, on the contrary, was too easygoing and indolent to look for anything in him but the indulgent consideration for her every whim which never failed.

"Grace has had everything to do with it, sir. She deluded the poor fellow into falling in love with her, and then sent him off in a pique."

"Well, I must say you are hard on the girl, Frank. How could she help him or any other fellow falling in love with her?

You would have done it yourself, man, had she been any one else's sister."

"Scarcely, I think : but Grace is perfection in your eyes, I know, sir, so there is no use in arguing the point."

"Not the slightest, Frank. Henry had very little to do to think of your sister for a moment. Your mother would never have heard of such a match for her, and I have a far better prospect in my head just at present for the poor girl—God bless her!"

"Anything new turned up, eh, sir?"

"Yes. I must say I was a little surprised when O'Brien broached the subject to me."

"Not Manus, surely? Why, he is as old as you, sir, if not older."

"Nonsense, Frank! Manus O'Brien is some years my junior, and I can tell you he's by no means to be despised as a speculation. There's no man in the country has so substantial a freehold at his back, and he's a right good fellow, too,—loyal and true to the backbone. What more could the girl want?"

"Well, if I was a girl, I'd like a younger man. However, Manus is not a bad fellow, and it would be a safe enough settlement for Grace. But I have an idea she has some other string to her bow, though I doubt if it's one to be trusted."

"How now, Frank! What do you mean?"

"It may be nothing, sir; only from a hint poor Henry gave me the last time I saw him, I fancy that fellow Ward has been installing himself rather into her good graces, and I question if he's all they took him for at Leagh."

"Ward, eh! He's younger, certainly, and the girl might take it into her head to fancy him; but, as you say, he may not be quite the right thing for Grace after all. You see, Frank, an adventurous spirit is all very well for a young man, but poor Manus's broad acres will yield more presentable black cattle than all Ward could get in a lifetime of preying."

"That is true, certainly, sir; but Grace will take her own way in the matter, I should say. We don't know how far this fellow Ward may have gone."

"Ah! but your mother, Frank, she will soon see how it is, and Grace is too wise a little woman to throw herself away on a pauper."

"Yes, Grace would never do for a poor man's wife. Perhaps Manus will be the thing after all; it would be a good enough position for Grace, to be mistress of Ballygany Castle."

"I am glad you see it in that light, Frank: to tell you the truth, I thought you would. I must get back to Leagh without delay, and see how the land lies."

"You came to my rescue just now, Scott," said Sarsfield, when Major Colthurst had moved away. "Those English fellows have no more notion of what we are thinking about than an infant: the idea of our settling ourselves down here under their yoke is rather preposterous. What is there for us in Ireland but fighting, and how can we fight without the means? But there must be ways and means somewhere for us, and we will work them out sooner or later; what do you say, Colonel? Ireland is surely not the place for you either, under the thraldom of the heretic."

"The heresy has not much to say to it as far as I am concerned: I let such things take their own course pretty much. Men will think differently about religion to the end of time, and they may be just as good friends into the bargain; but Ireland will be a sadly changed place for all of us, and I think with you we are as well out of her."

"For the present only, remember, Colonel."

"Yes, I know you look forward to a brighter day; but I am not so hopefully inclined, and for my part, once I leave Ireland, I doubt if I shall ever see her shores again."

"You are desponding, Scott: you have ties here, have you not? Why will you break them all so easily?"

"I have but few ties in the world: now this campaign is over, it matters little to me which way I turn."

" Your brother! What does he say to this?"

"Ah, Conn! It is different for him, he would do well to settle here, I tell him; any interest I have in our own country I intend making over to him."

"To induce him to abandon the cause, Colonel; how is that?"

" His going or staying will have but little weight one way or the other."

" That is the argument many will bring forward, I fear: even the wildest of the Rapparees, I hear, are submitting every day, and pledging themselves to become decent members of society under the new rule."

" You will be better without such fellows, I think, General; but is it true that Hogan has given in at last?"

" So I understand, and it's fellows of his spirit that we want to animate the others."

" You are likely to have him then, sir," said Frank Colthurst, who had joined them. " I hear the ruffian has announced his intention of following your fortunes across the seas. I can hardly wish you joy of such companionship."

"You do not know the stuff the fellow is made of, Colthurst; he is wild and untamed certainly, but he is as brave as a lion."

"Yes, he would shoot a fellow down as soon as look at him. I have some idea of his way of working, and I don't envy you your prize."

"Have you not come to a juster appreciation of the Irish character yet, Colthurst? Setting aside such specimens as Hogan, of course, the class he belongs to is one which civil war in any country must produce; but honestly now confess, has not this last campaign raised your opinion as to the quality of Irish soldiery?"

"Why, to tell you the truth, General, my opinion is not changed. I think of them very much as I always did: your niece exerted all her powers to bring me round to her way of thinking, when I was indebted to you for hospitality, but except to admire her enthusiasm, I was unmoved."

"Yes, I remember; Mary has not lost

her enthusiasm, I assure you, Colthurst, even with the turn events have taken, and believe me, meanly as you may and I daresay do think of us, change kings, I say, with us, and we will willingly try our luck with you again."

"I object to the proposal, certainly," said the young man. "William and James at the head of an army are not to be compared; you judge rightly there, Lord Lucan, and there would be no withstanding Miss Sarsfield's patriotism, I think, if she had King William at her back. May I have the honour of paying my respects to your ladies, General, to thank them for their treatment of me when I was dependent on you?"

"Certainly, certainly, Colthurst, and you will find my niece as undaunted as ever, I think."

"What did she say to the O'Donnell desertion, I wonder," thought Frank, as he turned away. "I am slightly curious on that head, strange to say."

CHAPTER XL.

"And the far wanderings of the soul in dreams,
Calling up shrouded faces from the dead."
MRS. HEMANS.

"Is that you, Isma? Dear me! where have you been all this time? It is so dark and cold: stir the fire, child, and do light the candles, it is so horribly gloomy and still here. There, that will do, don't flash the light in my eyes, it dazzles me. Where is mamma, and where have you been? One might as well live in a city of the dead as in this place." So spoke Grace Colthurst as her cousin came into the room one evening in the twilight.

"I thought aunt was here; I did not know you were alone, Grace, or I would have come down sooner," said Isma, as she obeyed her cousin's directions.

"There, that will do; can't you stir the fire without making such a noise, Isma? I have been asleep, I think, and am not half awake yet; such a disagreeable dream, too, as I have had, but indeed it's no wonder one should be dismal, living in such a place with no one to speak to."

"The evenings get dark so soon now: I had no idea it was so late. Who has been troubling you in your dreams, Grace?"

"Oh, Guy of course. I do believe he was brought into the world purposely to trouble me. Why on earth did he make such a fuss the last time he was here. His face has haunted me ever since, and now I dreamt that he was in danger, and that he called to me and looked just as he did the other evening, and when I turned away he said, 'False, false.' I awoke then, I suppose, for I found myself alone in this dreary room, and the shadows seemed creeping round me. I felt so frightened, Isma: you can't think how disagreeable it was. I never was so glad to see any one as I was when you opened the door. What is that noise? Oh, it is only rain, I believe: what a dark night it is, and how it does rain," she said, as she looked out, and listened to the heavy pelting of the rain against the window.

"It has set in for a regular wet night, I think," said Isma: "what a pity of any one obliged to be out. It is so dark and cold, too."

"Yes, I wonder where that poor Guy is. I declare I think he deserves to be out, and drenched too, for giving me such horrid dreams. I shall never forget how he looked as I thought I saw him; and his voice, oh, I hear it still; why should he say I was false, Isma? Speak, child, do; why are you so silent," she urged, as Isma paused ere she answered.

"I was thinking what to say, Grace. You see, I don't know exactly how it was between you and him, and I was so sorry that night when I saw him go."

"You think, then, that perhaps I was false: is that it, Isma?"

"I do not mean that: you would not—you could not have intended to deceive him."

"What a simpleton you are, Isma,

talking of deceiving, and looking so earnest all about nothing."

"I did not think it was nothing; you spoke as if you really cared, a moment ago."

"I am sure I do not care to have such a dream, and then to see your face half a yard long when I asked you a simple question."

"But I thought it was a serious question, Grace."

"Yes, but I did not want a serious answer in return; of course you can't know anything about it, I only want you to talk, and say something to drive away the horrid sensations I have had in that dream. I know I wish that some one would come to break this dreadful monotony."

"I wonder when Captain Henry will come again," said Isma.

"Oh, soon enough I dare say, and it's to be hoped he'll be in a better humour than the last time, when he does come; it really was very unfortunate he got so angry with me, and I am sure I could not help his liking me so much; now could I, Isma?"

"I don't know, Grace; did he not think you liked him too?"

"Of course I liked him, we were always good friends, and I do not see why one cannot be pleasant to people without their throwing it up in your face afterwards, as if you had done some harm."

"You did not mean any harm, I am sure, Grace, but it may have been great harm to him."

"Well, I do not see that I am accountable for it: Guy should have known I could never have married him; love is all very well, but I never could love any one well enough to try what poverty was like in his company, and that's just the truth of it, Isma."

"Well, then, it is as well for him you were not tempted, for I should think poverty would require a good deal of love to make it bearable in any case."

"Yes, that's just what I think, and I have made up my mind all along not to try what love in a cottage would be like: that would suit you better, Isma. You are just the romantic sort of little creature that would fall into a rapture, and scorn the idea that it was necessary to bestow a thought on the ways and means; is it not so, child? Ah, how you blush: mother, here is this child acknowledging that she needs nothing but true love to thrive on."

"Nonsense, Grace; why will you put such ideas into the girl's head? I am sure she has seen quite enough misery already to keep her from following her mother's example in that particular."

"I do not know what you mean, Aunt; my father and mother were not miserable, certainly. I remember well how happy they were together."

"Well, I cannot understand how that could be, my dear. Your mother was brought up with every comfort and luxury, which I am sure could not have fallen to her lot much in after-life."

"But, Aunt, do you think happiness depends on such things?"

"Some people have the spirit and energy to rise above such things, my dear, but your poor mother was of an entirely different nature. She was quite too delicate to fight her way in the world, and of course your father could not understand her refined sensibilities: how could he? She was altogether such a contrast to any one he had ever been associated with previously. It is a great mistake in marriage for people to step out of the position Providence has placed them in. You need not look so angry, my dear. No one is blaming you about it, but it cannot be denied that your father and mother were unsuited to each other by birth and religion, and indeed in every particular. She was curiously self-willed in the matter for one usually so gentle, but of course it was all his influence, and I trust, my dear, it will be a lesson to you not to allow yourself to be influenced and led away by any one who is not naturally competent to judge in such a matter for you."

"You forget, Aunt, that my mother

must have been influenced by her love for my father, and I do not think to the end she ever repented having given up everything for him: if you could only have known how devoted he was to her, you would not think they were so unsuitable to each other."

"You can know nothing about it, my dear. Unfortunately you have too much of your father's nature in you to understand what a false step your mother made in her marriage, and the love you talk so glibly of was only the result of pride on his part and obstinacy on hers; but it is quite unprofitable to go over the past in this way, it cannot be altered. I only speak of it because I felt that it was my duty to let you know my opinion on the subject."

"Mamma lives in terror, you see, Isma, of your going and doing likewise some time or other. But indeed, mother mine, I can tell you, you may as well save yourself the trouble; the child has her mind made up that there's nothing like love to eat, drink, and sleep upon. Your advice is far better bestowed upon me, I always listen to reason, and, do you know, it was partly in consideration of your feelings I allowed poor Guy to go off in distraction that last night he was here: not that I could by any possibility boast of having a shadow of what Isma would call love for him in my composition; but it was so pleasant to know he thought me perfection and all that, and he was so innocent and unsophisticated, poor fellow! How that dream haunts me! Dear me, I think I will go to bed, and try and sleep off the effects of it. Good night, mother; don't be too hard on Isma. It is her nature to believe in romance, you know, as it is for yours and mine to be prosaic and coldblooded. Come along, Isma, to bed, I'd advise you: it's no use contending against the stream," she whispered; " besides I want your company to-night, or I shall not sleep a wink, I know, listening to that wind and rain." And so the evening passed with Grace,—the evening when Guy went out unconsciously to meet his death, and the rain which she listened to so heedlessly washed the blood stains from his weary upturned face, and the noise of the wind, which filled her with vague fancies, sighed and whistled over his head as he lay alone all quiet and calm under the dark starless sky.

CHAPTER XLI.

> "No.
> I was the one who wronged our truth—I, I.
> He was all truth."—A. WEBSTER.

It was not many days after this that Isma came with a pale, horror-stricken face to her cousin.

"What is it, Isma? You have heard some news—my father or Frank? Speak, child?"

"I have heard nothing about them, but oh, Grace! Your dream, do you remember? He was in danger and ——"

"What do you mean, Isma? My dream—what dream, child?—was in danger—— Do speak plainly."

"Do you not remember, Grace," said Isma more quietly, "a dream you had some evenings ago about Captain Henry. You said you saw him in some danger."

"Yes, to be sure I do, but what of it?—and what of him?"

"He was in danger that night, Grace; the man who was with him is here."

"Was in danger, you say; but it is past now. How strange I should dream about it. What does the man say? Where is Guy now?"

"The danger is past, Grace, for him. He will never trouble you with his love again."

"Do you mean that he is dead, Isma?" And Grace shuddered as she spoke, and for a moment a deadly paleness came over her face.

"Yes, dear, it was a bullet. He could not have suffered much."

"And it is true; he will never come back here again—never. Oh, Isma, why did I let him go? I shall never forget his face as I saw it in my dream. It will haunt me always. Guy, poor Guy, so it is all over with you, and I have done it. I have sent you away to die. Oh, it is horrible, horrible, Isma;" and in a burst of real feeling the girl threw herself on a couch.

"You could not have helped it, Grace dear. You could not have shielded him from this danger, even if you had loved him."

"He would not have gone, he would not have sought this danger, as I fear he did, if I had not let him go away in anger. Oh! Isma, Isma, why did I let him care so much for me?"

"It is your nature to make people care for you, I suppose, Cousin, and after all, when you could not give him back the love he felt for you, perhaps he is happier as it is, poor fellow. He had not to bear trouble long, he died doing his duty, the man says. It is Cunningham, the drummer; he was with him and another soldier who fell with Captain Henry."

"What is this, Grace? What is this news I hear?" said Mrs. Colthurst in her usually cold, measured tone. "They tell me Captain Henry has been shot. Very dreadful, certainly, but such things will happen in time of war. It is very startling, very, particularly when the young man was so lately with us; but you know, Grace, it is scarcely becoming to indulge in such an excess of feeling for any one who was not bound to us by any ties of relationship or otherwise. Indeed, my dear, I feel it is a cause for great thankfulness that it was not either your father or poor Frank who met with this misfortune."

"Certainly, mamma, but Guy has been our friend for so long, and I feel so remorseful for the way in which we parted the last time he was here: he cared for me so much, you don't know how much, mamma, and I let him go away in anger. I am very, very sorry, mother; you may say what you like now, but he was only too good and true for me: all these years that he has thought of me, and I kept him on, I know I did, though I never meant to marry him. Yes, you may look reproachfully at me, Isma, I couldn't help it, it was so pleasant to be admired and cared for, as I knew he cared for me. I have been false, he was right, and now I never can undo it."

"Grace! I am surprised at you; have you no control over yourself? Isma, you must have put these notions into your cousin's head. She is usually so reasonable: this is absurd, you know, Grace; it would have been strange if the young man had not admired you, as every one does, and his doing so or not could not affect this unfortunate occurrence one way or another."

"Isma has nothing whatever to do with it, mamma: don't scold her, and you may spare me too, for I will not trouble you with a scene any longer, but for all that I would give worlds to have poor Guy back for one moment, just to see him go away with a happy face, poor fellow! He deserved some one far better than me. Let me go alone, Isma," she said, as she saw her cousin preparing to follow her from the room. "I will get over it soon, but I would have been a stick or a stone if I did not feel the shock of this a little."

She did feel it, in her own way, it was true, selfish and worldly though she was by nature and bringing up. She had no intention to bring misfortune on another, and the thought of her old playmate gone for ever, and gone from her in anger and trouble, filled her for the time with remorse, but as yet her heart had not been stirred to love deeply any one except her own small person. Neither could her sorrow, sincere even for the moment, last much beyond that moment; the cloud passed over her, and a cloud it was surely as it passed; but it left scarcely a shadow behind. As strongly as before, the ever present thought of self and self-interest, with all its hopes and fears in their paramount influence, shone out, and Guy and his trouble, and his sad death, passed from the scene; and left but a faint memory of regret behind.

CHAPTER XLII.

"Ne'er with an Englishman in friendship be;
Should'st thou be so t'will be the worse for thee."
Old Irish Song.

"I HAVE not intruded upon you, Miss Sarsfield, without permission from your uncle to pay my respects to you and Lady Lucan," said Frank Colthurst, some days after the treaty had been finally signed and sealed between the hostile armies. He had made his way to the same old house in the city of Limerick where he had passed some weeks a year ago as Sarsfield's prisoner after the encounter at Ballyneedy.

A haughty inclination of the head was the only answer the young lady vouchsafed to give, and Frank, who was by no means easy to baffle, was left to continue the conversation.

"There have been great changes since you entertained me as your guest by courtesy, but in reality as your prisoner, in this room, Miss Sarsfield. The time has been a weary one to you, I dare say, though you do think there is no place to compare with Limerick in the world."

"How do you know that, Mr. Colthurst? Our long residence here lately has, as you know, been compulsory."

"Yes; but it is from your own words I drew this inference of your preference for Limerick. Do you not remember; or have the important events of the past year totally blotted from your memory the arguments we had together when we met first?"

"I remember the contemptuous sneers, certainly, which you indulged freely in at our expense, and I suppose they provoked me to defend our poor town."

"You are as severe on us as ever, I see, Miss Sarsfield. For my part, I remember your enthusiastic defence, but I cannot recal those disagreeable sneers you allude to. On the contrary, I think I was inclined to urge you to drop the party animosity, and forget for a while that we were *enemies*, as you chose to call us."

"Your memory is wonderfully correct, certainly, Mr. Colthurst. I remember objecting to any compromise of the real state of the case: you wanted to persuade me that we could forget our respective prejudices, and set up a sort of platonic friendship, based on nothing, not even old association."

"Could we have nothing in common, then, between us? You are harder than ever, Miss Sarsfield. What have I done to merit such severity?"

"I do not mean to be particularly severe on you, Mr. Colthurst, for I am not sufficiently acquainted with you to warrant any such judgment. But it is the idea that you put forward I raise my voice against. We could not bridge over the wide gulf between us by a hollow feint of friendship. For me, at least, it would be almost impossible."

"Well, that was all very fair the last time we met, but now things are different. You do not mean to keep up those insuperable barriers that divided us in your eyes before?"

"Yes, circumstances are very much changed,—different altogether for us; but my opinions are the same, Mr. Colthurst. Ireland and her wrongs will ever be the uppermost thought in my mind; and, as I dare say Ireland is as little to you as England is to me, it is not likely that our interests could be at all the same."

"You are very much mistaken, Miss Sarsfield. I am deeply interested in this country, as I shall most probably pass the greater part of my life here; but I am afraid we should scarcely agree as to her wrongs. For my part, I am blind to see what is wrong with her now that this miserable war is at an end. Why cannot we all settle down and pull amicably together, as they do in England, where there is as much diversity of opinion as here, if the truth were told?"

"It is hard to forget that we are slaves with the chains about our necks still, and the blood of our fallen countrymen calling for vengeance. We cannot forget the past, Mr. Colthurst, and, what is more, we will not. It is very well for you to talk of peace when you are the conquerors, when you have crushed us even to the earth, and pulled down all our strongholds of faith and loyalty. It is not quite so easy for us to gather ourselves up and cover the chains you have bound us in with flowers, and look for peace to your cold, passionless faith, and bow down to the usurper's power you have chosen to raise above us. No, it cannot be; natures like ours are not thus quickly changed, Mr. Colthurst."

"Are they not?" said the young man, with the sneer he could scarcely repress. " No one ever breaks faith in your ranks, I suppose; no one ever raises your hopes with prophetic dreams which he comes so gloriously to fulfil, and which vanish away like one of his own castles in Spain before you can realize them. Ah, no! brave words are never spoken in Ireland in your ears to-day and eaten to-morrow in humble pie across the Channel. I do not wonder at your enthusiasm, Miss Sarsfield: how could it be otherwise when you have such heroes as the Baldearg on your side. We cannot boast such men of valour and honour among our numbers."

A deep flush of anger spread over the girl's face, and she answered quickly.

"You are cruel—crueller than I thought, Mr. Colthurst. Let us alone; spare us your scorn at least."

"Pardon me, Miss Sarsfield. I did not think you would have taken the O'Donnell affair so much to heart."

"You did know—you must have known that such things are the bitterest part of our misfortune; and, what is more, you have lent your hand to the work, too. I know your party designed and contrived his ruin, and then you come with fair words of friendship. Can you wonder that I am bitter—hard, if you will—against you?"

"You do not know whom to trust, Miss Sarsfield. If you could be induced to remember that it is with the sincerest view for the good of your country that we do these things, you would see the matter in a different light."

"I do not want to see it in a different light. I do not want to be guided in my judgment by your opinion. You are all strangers and aliens. We hate you and the policy you would force upon us: how can we trust you when you make us distrust each other, when you intrigue and plot against us, not only yourselves, but with us against ourselves."

"You have excited yourself with this controversy, Miss Sarsfield. I have made you angry, when it was in reality my purpose to conciliate you, if it had been possible."

"You took rather an odd way to do so, then, I must say, Mr. Colthurst. Your scornful taunts were scarcely conciliatory, as you must have known; but it has shown me more clearly than ever that I was right in refusing to acknowledge any possibility of friendship between us. You see yourself, now, the gulf that separates us."

"Still, I would bridge it over. Your enthusiasm is infectious, Miss Sarsfield, and you do not know what you could make of me. Tolerate me only, and you will perhaps find me a willing worshipper at your patriotic shrine in the end. You do not know what admiration such pure-minded enthusiasm as yours can kindle in a cold-blooded creature like me. I have offended you, but you will forgive me this time, and let me persevere in my claim for friendship at least."

"We have both been to blame for entering upon such a hopeless and unprofitable argument, and I think, Mr. Colthurst, you had better seek for some other enthusiast than me to provoke your cold blood. This is probably the last time we shall meet, as of course I accompany my uncle to France, and we are not likely to come across each other there, fortunately for my temper at least."

"Why will you not direct your enthusiasm to induce your uncle not to desert his country in this way?"

"Because I do not consider it desertion, and I long to find myself far away for a time from the scene of so much misfortune and unhappiness."

"And from those who have caused it?" said Colthurst, his cold eye glittering with the disappointment he felt that for once in his life he had failed in making an undying impression on any one whom he had condescended to admire.

"Yes," she said, honestly, "my prejudices are too strong, as you know, to allow me to be reasonable with any one on your side, and I think for a time at least we need a cessation from useless warfare, even in words." Frank could say no more; he had admired the girl, but there was not a spark of admiration for him in the beautiful dark grey eyes which she turned for an instant towards him as they parted.

CHAPTER XLIII.

"It is success that colours all in life."
                                THOMSON.

MARY SARSFIELD had keenly felt the result of the long struggle which, throughout, she had watched with such jealous eyes. Her romantic, ardent nature had seen in the Baldearg the long-looked-for hero, and his withdrawal from the scene had shattered the idol she had almost unconsciously raised for herself, and broken the spell which in the short time they had been thrown together he had cast over her. Bitterly and sadly she went over the scenes in which he had stood forth as the champion of his country, and contrasted them with the scornful picture Frank Colthurst had drawn. Yes, it was only too true, prophetic dreams were still unfulfilled, the promises unrealized.

"You are alone, Miss Sarsfield?" said a quiet voice at her side, interrupting the train of thought which filled her mind, as she sat still where Colthurst had left her.

"Yes, Colonel Scott, my uncle is out. He is more occupied than ever with the people. Will he succeed, think you, in inducing them to leave Ireland with us?"

"I fear only in a limited degree. The fact is, the people do not understand the state of the case. They are tired out and hopeless after the long struggle, and have no heart to look forward."

"Yes, I am sure that is it. They are offered peace and quiet here, and we have nothing but an uncertain future to put before them."

"Nothing else indeed, and we Irish are not fond of leaving our native sod, even though it may have thorns in plenty for us to lie upon."

"Still, you are going yourself. You have not changed your mind, surely?"

"No, I go myself, no matter who goes; but I can sympathize with those who feel indisposed to break the ties which bind them to Ireland. It is easy enough for us to go, Miss Sarsfield, when it does not entail leaving the only spot of land in the whole world we can look upon as home; leaving, too, wives or children to get on as best they may, with no sure prospect of ever meeting again."

"Yes, this would be hard, but my uncle has plans to transport whole families if they will only come. His great idea is to bring over a sufficient number to discipline into a regular brigade, which he hopes to make good use of at a future time."

"Yes, I know, and if any man could do it, he will. His energy seems never once to have failed all this weary time." With a tired, sad voice Edward Scott spoke, and his companion looked curiously at him. His face was always quiet, but the last few months had deepened the lines of care, and shadowed over the bright eyes with a tender, wistful look.

"My uncle is very strong, but why is it that he has not succeeded?"

"Why is it that none of us ever seem to succeed in this world?" said the Colonel.

"But some do. Some people never appear to know what failure is. I often wonder how they manage to conceal their skeletons so carefully away."

"Then you believe that in spite of this appearance of success, every one must have some skeleton in his heart?"

"I suppose they must have, but they cover it up with self-satisfaction in some wonderful way, so that no one could discover what it is. I think the English are particularly clever in this matter; they are so perfectly satisfied with themselves, and they expect every one else to be quite as well pleased as they are."

"And do you think we poor Irish fail in this respect?"

"Yes, generally, if we are unhappy, we can rarely hide it, from our friends at least: now I think you are not quite happy about leaving Ireland; is it not so, Colonel Scott?"

He started: could his quiet voice tell any tale of trouble: he had thought it impossible.

"Do you think you have come across my skeleton, Miss Sarsfield?" he said, with a faint smile.

"Pardon me, it is wrong of me to have spoken thus; but you spoke so sadly just now I could not help thinking you were leaving Ireland only because you thought it was your duty."

"No; I am afraid my going to France is entirely selfish. I have none of the ties I spoke of to keep me in this country, and I particularly wish to leave a place where we have all met with such disappointments."

"Yes, I am afraid none of us can conceal that the skeleton of disappointment has a corner in all our hearts."

"You are too young to take such a skeleton to your heart, Miss Sarsfield; you have been deeply interested in Ireland, I know, but life in France will have many sources of pleasure for you, and you will soon find this skeleton crumble away into dust."

"I am not quite so sure of that, Colonel Scott; it is hard to lay the ghost of a skeleton, even when time has crumbled it away, as you say. But your brother, Colonel Scott, is he not a tie in this country for you? I think I heard you say he would not leave with you?"

"No, he hopes not to do so, and I am afraid your uncle thinks I am sadly deserting the cause, by not urging Conn to come with us; but the truth is, I am doing all I can to induce him to remain here."

"Why do you like to leave him? He will scarcely be content to stay."

"That depends entirely on circumstances, and, much as I shall miss him, I think it is the best thing for him to do."

"Will he be quite alone, then?"

"He hopes not," said the Colonel, his quiet tone even quieter than before. "In fact he hopes to win a wife for himself, and settle down near our old home in the North. We have an old cousin, too, whom I wish him to be near; she has been good and kind to us, and it would be a trouble to me to think of her alone in her old age."

"Your brother seems very young to settle down. I wonder it is not he that is going to seek his fortune in a new country, while you go back to your old home? I wonder you have never married, Colonel Scott?"

"Do you think me so very antiquated, then, Miss Sarsfield," said he, while the shadow grew darker on his brow. "I do not wonder you should think it strange that I am still a wandering vagabond on the face of the earth without ties or home, but a soldier is better without such things, and at any rate fate has willed it so."

"Perhaps it will not be so always!" she said, her quick eyes detecting the trouble in his face.

"Yes, I am afraid, so—always," he answered quietly. "I think there is no chance of my skeleton crumbling away to a ghost, as I prophesy will be the fate of yours," he added with an effort at playfulness, which she answered in the same tone.

"We shall see; perhaps my skeleton is the toughest of the two, after all."

"Here you are, Scott," said the Earl, joining them hastily. "You are just the man I want to see; did you hear that Ginkel has put forth proclamations in every direction, promising all who settle down here any amount of protection and favour. To those who wish for service, King William's ranks are open to them all, while those who choose to enlist under Louis' banner must make up their minds to banishment from their native land for good and all."

"What do the people say to it?"

"Oh! they are divided as usual, and it is necessary for us to use some active means to influence them. I am thinking of using the clergy in the business: let them put it to the fellows as desertion of the Church, for so in fact it will be. Once this dynasty is fairly established here, we may say good-bye to our ancient worship. The new creeds will gradually creep in with the usurper's power, and, religious distinctions gone, the mass of the people care very little whether their king's name is James or William."

" But, Uncle, the Church will stand by its own power; you do not fear for her, surely," said Mary.

"She cannot stand if the fates are against her. It is impossible. Means must be used in everything."

" Ireland can never give up her ancient faith, Uncle. It could not be. A remnant will still be found as a witness."

" We must try and help her, Mary; we must come back ourselves in good time, and gather in the remnant. And now, Colonel, I must ask you to come with me; there is much to be done and thought of still."

" Farewell for the present, then, Miss Sarsfield, and do not fear but that God's truth, in whatever Church it may be, will withstand all storms."

CHAPTER XLIV.

"And yet, believe me, good as well as ill,
Woman's at best a contradiction still."

POPE.

"WHAT reward will you give me, Miss Colthurst, for bringing you the good news of the capitulation?"

"Did you do it for a reward, Captain Ward? I flattered myself it was a purely disinterested piece of good nature on your part, or that perhaps you found it a convenient way for putting in a little spare time."

They paced up and down a broad walk which ran round the walls of the Bawn at Leagh, shaded by trees which at each movement of the wind let fall a shower of yellowing leaves on the path.

"You were slightly mistaken for once, Miss Colthurst; I most certainly did it for a reward, and one that you can neither give nor withhold—one that I must take for myself; one, in fact, that I am taking now."

" The privilege of being at Leagh, then, must have been your goal."

" Certainly, and you can pretty well guess, too, that Leagh is nothing to me without something else."

" No, I don't suppose you would come very far out of your way to see these old trees, or the ugly grey walls that make the house seem like a real prison, as it is too, just at present."

" It is a lightsome enough prison to me, I hope I may never see the inside of a darker one. But I do not wonder it is dreary enough to you; you were meant for brighter scenes than the last months have brought you, shut up here. However, it is over, and now that this war is over indeed, you may look forward to emancipation."

" Yes, no one could be more glad than I am that it is over. Such terrible things have happened, and we never knew what we might hear next."

"You allude to poor Henry's death perhaps," he said, closely scanning her face, which was grave and quiet for the moment.

"I do. It was a shock to me; we had known each other so long."

"It was unfortunate: but a fellow might almost be tempted to go in for such a thing if he knew you could look so sorrowful, so tender, as you thought of him."

"I am sorry for him, but I do not know that I could get up my compassion to order for any one else, Captain Ward, in the same way."

"You don't mean to say you would not have bestowed one kind thought on my memory, for instance, had it been my fate, instead of Henry's, to fall?"

"You forget he was an old friend, Captain Ward; you I know but a few weeks at the most."

"Ah! but it is not time that does such things; we were friends in a day."

"Were we? I was scarcely aware of it."

"Oh, no, that is the beauty of it. We understood each other at once, in an unconscious way that quits one of the trouble of those endless years of probation some people think proper to go through. You don't like much trouble, I think, and neither do I; so, you see, it suits us just to take up our friendship somewhat on trust."

"I am not quite sure that I understand you at all, Captain Ward; you run on in such a wild incoherent fashion, there is no knowing exactly what you mean."

"Do I? Well, you must teach me to be more coherent; you understood me pretty well just now about the reward I set before myself in paying you this visit, yet we have not quite settled that point either, I think."

"I thought you needed no other reward than to feel yourself under the shadow of the Bawn. What more can we settle, or rather what more can you want?"

"Well, for the present I don't think I do want much more, so long as you will let me hear your voice, and now and then, please, you must look up—yes, in that way. I need light, you know, sometimes, now the sun is going down."

"How absurd you are, Captain Ward! No wonder I look up in amazement."

"That is exactly what I want, and if you like we will go on gradually, and become old friends in days—years we must dispense with—life is too uncertain for such loss of time. Do you not think so?"

"I think you have talked enough nonsense for some little time, so we had better go in; the sun has gone long ago."

"Nonsense! friendship is not nonsense, is it, Miss Colthurst?"

"Friendship? no. But I think we agreed before this that friendship was too formidable a thing for you or me to undertake. It involves a good deal, you see,—qualities which I for one have no claim to."

"But I thought you acknowledged the advantage an old friend had just now, when it came to your feelings for him in the end."

"Yes, but it is troublesome, the sort of bondage you must be in to a friend."

"Well, all I ask is, let me come and

go, and find you just as you may happen to be, and time will tell whether we turn out friends or foes."

"Very well. But remember I am fickle, not more to be depended upon than those withered leaves which are blown about in every direction by the wind. See how they dance along the path, and how they get caught in some corner where even the wind can't root them out for one more dance. How cold it has got; come, I must go in. Some one has come. Can it be father or Frank, I wonder," she continued as they drew near the house.

Major Colthurst had arrived; and for some time Captain Ward found himself forgotten in the excitement of the home coming. The major had recognised and greeted him with rather constrained politeness, and at the first opportunity of being alone with his wife he cross-questioned her curiously about her guest.

"I thought you had met him yourself, my dear Major; you surely ought to know more about the young man than I can do."

"Yes, Frank introduced him to me one day at head-quarters, and I exchanged a few words with him. I can't say I know much about him, nor Frank either as far as I could gather, but from some remarks I heard between him and another officer, it struck me there was something to be known about this fellow Ward."

"Indeed; somehow I thought you or Frank knew him intimately. He was laid up here, as I told you, after some fray. Grace and I found him most agreeable, and altogether I thought there was an air of distinction and position about him which could not be mistaken."

"Just so. You women always judge a man by his face or his walk, or some such accident. If a man holds up his head and turns out his toes, you say he is an officer and a gentleman, and that is quite enough."

"Have you any reason to think Captain Ward is neither an officer nor a gentleman?" said Mrs. Colthurst, coldly.

"I can't say I have, my dear. But can

you tell me who he is or what he is, and I'm sure I've no objection in life that you should admire him as much as ever you like. He is a fine-looking young fellow, I grant you, and Grace may take it into her pretty head to admire him rather too much, you see."

"And what of that, Major? If he is what I understand he is, I am sure we ought not to stand in Grace's way of a good settlement."

"That's just the point, my dear. What do you understand the fellow is, and would it be a good settlement?"

"I have taken care to consider this, as it is only right to be cautious in such matters, and, as far as I can learn, the young man has property and position in the North; and of course I expected that you or Frank would know all about him. Indeed, Frank is sure to be able to throw some light on the subject. He is never at a loss to form a correct opinion."

"You're right, my dear, the lad's too like his mother, God bless her, not to know what's what. We'll wait till Frank comes to see how the matter stands; but what do you think is Grace's opinion on the subject? Perhaps it's too late to say anything."

"Nonsense, Major; Grace never forgets herself. She likes Captain Ward well enough, I dare say, but I think we can trust her not to commit herself in any way."

"Well, I am glad of that, for you must know there is another prospect open for the girl, if you and she think well of it."

"Dear me, how odd you are, Major. Why did you not tell me about this, whatever it is, at once?"

"Patience, my dear; I thought it well to see how the land lay first at home, and I'm not so sure of how you'll take this proposal. It is not to be despised, I think myself. Poor Manus has too many broad acres at his back for a girl to turn up her nose at him."

"Manus! whom do you mean, Major? Not O'Brien of Ballygany, surely?"

"The same, my dear, and a right good fellow he is, though, to be sure, a trifle too old for Grace, if it could be helped."

" Well, I never would have guessed such a thing. Ballygany! It's not to be despised certainly, as you say, but, Major, what made him think of Grace so suddenly?"

" Why, it seems that he admired the girl always, but had an idea in his head that she and that poor fellow Henry were to make a match of it, and when he heard of his death he thought, that obstacle being removed, he might as well put in a claim. He is a liberal, generous fellow, and for my part I don't see how Grace could do better. He's a strong hardy man, too, and may live long enough; who knows? I'm only afraid she may turn rusty about it. You know he's scarcely the man a girl would fancy of her own free will."

"Grace is wonderfully sensible, and I think if it is put in a proper light before her, she will see the advantages she would gain by such a match."

" You are not afraid of this fellow Ward, then ?"

" No, I think not. To be sure Grace does take fancies occasionally, but I think in the end her sense would carry the day. I must sound her on the subject, and see what can be done."

"All right, my dear. Remember, I leave it entirely in your hands."

CHAPTER XLV.

"In life can love be bought with gold."
JOHNSON.

MAJOR COLTHURST was an easy-going, good-natured man, and his kind manner soon put Isma more at her ease with him than she ever was with her aunt and cousin.

"Uncle," she said one day not long after his return home, "I think you said you had met Colonel Scott among the Irish officers."

"I did, my dear, and a gentlemanly fine fellow he seems to be, too. He is a friend of yours, your aunt told me. I did not know at the time, or I would have asked him here."

"Oh, uncle, thank you, but I am afraid he would not come. Did you hear him speak of his plans at all; will he be likely to go back to Sligo?"

"I should say not; indeed, I heard him speak as if he meant to go with Sarsfield to France."

"To France! Oh, do you think he will do that?"

"Most likely, my dear. A great many of them are turning their faces away from the old country; after all their fighting they can't rest at home. You look troubled, child; what is it?"

"I do not like to hear of my friends going away, uncle, that is all," said Isma, with a pale face.

"Friends, did you say, child? Ah, yes, Scott has a brother, I believe; I suppose he'll go with him. But maybe I'm upon a false scent after all; perhaps they're not on the run. We'll see about it, little girl, if you care to know."

"Please do, uncle; I care very much. Colonel Scott has been such a friend to me; he was my father's friend, too, you know."

"All right, child, I'll see about it when I go back to quarters. Don't trouble yourself, little one," he said kindly; "we'll take care of you, even if they go off. I remember your father right well; he was a brave soldier, and that is enough for me."

Captain Ward did not remain much longer at Leagh, but long enough to see that in the novelty of the Major's return a stranger's presence was scarcely desired. He left without hesitation, pretty certain that with Grace, at least, his return would be looked for, and thought of as in the natural course of events.

Mrs. Colthurst was not sorry to find herself free from his presence, for she began to doubt her prudence in allowing him to become so intimate with Grace, now that there was a probability of her becoming mistress of no less a place than Ballygany Castle. "After all, what do I know certainly about this young man?" she thought. "There is no doubt he has a most presentable appearance, but that is not sufficient in the long run by any means. Now, Ballygany Castle is a reality, there is no mistake. I must see what Grace will think about it. I do hope the girl will not be a fool; I am sure she frightened me quite enough about poor Guy Henry, and after all I don't think she cared much for him."

An opportunity soon occurred for her to find out somewhat of Grace's ideas on the subject, Grace herself opening the conversation one day by a sudden question.

"Mother, what does father think of Captain Ward? I did not think he was very cordial to him, did you?"

"Well, my dear, your father was here such a short time with him I had hardly opportunity to judge."

"But did he not make any remark with regard to him, mother?"

"He was surprised to find him so intimate here, I think; but he didn't seem to know much about him."

"Frank knows him, I am sure, and I wonder father did not ask Captain Ward to stay longer."

"Perhaps it is as well he did not. You see, Grace, we really do not know much of Captain Ward."

"What more do we want to know, mother?

I am sure he is the most agreeable person we have seen of late, and you used to like him very much; what is the meaning of this change?"

"There is no change that I am aware of, my dear; I only think that it would be as well to know a little more of Captain Ward's position and circumstances."

"Before I lose my heart to him, you mean, mother; I thought you were quite satisfied before that he was not a bad speculation."

"How you do talk, Grace! How can I know what the young man has or has not?"

"I'm sure I don't know, but you told me I might turn my attention to him if I liked."

"Nonsense, Grace; but I think you agreed with me that some little forethought in such matters was necessary."

"Certainly, mother, I have no fancy for pauperism."

"Well, then, I can tell you that if you choose it, you need never be afraid of that."

"Why, mother, has Captain Ward a fortune?"

"I was not thinking of Captain Ward, my dear, but there is another prospect before you. What would you think of becoming lady of Ballygany Castle?"

"Ballygany! Mother, what an idea! Why, Mr. O'Brien is as old as the hills!"

"But for all that he does not think you are too young for him. He wants you, Grace, to help him to do the honours of the castle."

"Me, mother! It is my turn to say nonsense now; the old dotard, what on earth should I do with him?"

"He would take care of you, my dear, and your father says there is no one in the country has such broad lands to boast of. We know what an old family the O'Briens are, and the castle is in a good state of preservation."

"Ah, this is the reason you are doubtful about Captain Ward, I see, mother. So you and father have concocted this little plan for me. Very well it sounds, too. I am dazzled in fact. But oh! mother, what could have made the man grow so old?"

"He is not so old as you think, dear. Your father says——"

"There, mother, please, that will do. I have heard enough for one day."

"But you will consider of it, Grace, dear?"

"Certainly, mother; only give me time to collect my wits again. It's quite too important a matter to be lightly considered. Think of all the reverence poor dear old Manus' years will entail upon my devoted head."

Grace Colthurst was in truth sorely perplexed in her mind: this new turn her prospects had taken was so unexpected that she found herself utterly unprepared to decide what course to take. Her father's old friend, Manus O'Brien, she had known all her life, but the idea of his marrying any one, much less herself, whom he had always looked upon as a child, had never entered her head. She had quizzed him, laughed with him, and amused him, unconscious that in her natural light-hearted merriment, the middle-aged, reserved man, who might have been her father, was craving for her youth and beauty to grace his dreary, old-fashioned castle-home, where he had lived all his life solitary, and secluded with a widowed mother. She was dead now, and the fact was borne in on her son's mind that it was his duty to perpetuate the noble family of O'Brien. Grace was young, pretty and lively. Would she not fill the place of Lady of Ballygany Castle to perfection? In his visits to Leagh Bawn he had noticed the attentions of Guy Henry to the girl, and, fearing the younger lover would be more acceptable to her, he had not ventured on proposing his plans. Guy could not stand in his way any longer now, and he had lost no time in expressing his wishes to the Major.

"What would she do?" That was the question which haunted her mind. To be mistress of the castle and the fortune of its master ought certainly to satisfy her ambitious desires—desires which from her babyhood had been instilled into her mind, till she had set them before her as the one object of life. But would the offered position and wealth satisfy her? The unchanging love of Guy Henry had left her heart-whole, but would it always be so? Would she never know the intensity of a love such as his had been for her? She had always scoffed at such love, ridiculed it; but now that he had gone, when his passionate love was silent for ever, she felt that it was not a thing to mock at, that with him at least it had been a reality. Was her nature so totally different that she could never feel what he had felt so keenly? She had always boasted that it was so, and in truth her love of self was so strong that it was doubtful if it could ever be absorbed in love for another. Still, why did the remembrance of one voice and the touch of one hand recur again and again to her mind? Could they have any more powerful fascination for her than any other voice or hand? And why did a sense of injustice rise up in her mind when she recalled the words her mother had spoken of their doubtful knowledge of Captain Ward? Why should they doubt him, or turn from his friendship, as if it was dangerous? His years apart, Manus O'Brien was unobjectionable in himself; he was kind, and would be indulgent, she knew, to her every wish; but could she give up her girlish life of freedom, and miss nothing in a life of ease and luxury with him?

Grace had never reasoned so seriously with herself before, and yet the conclusion seemed as far off as ever. One moment a vision of herself installed in dignity and honour at Ballygany seemed more than sufficient for her every wish. And then again, what would they all be compared to the fascination of a half-hour with a pair of dark eyes bent down upon her with that strange light in them which seemed to hold her enthralled, while the low voice, modulated to catch her ear only, whispered vague hints of an admiration which could not be concealed?

CHAPTER XLVI.

"'Twere somewhat dear to barter youth's bright days
For the cheap flattery of a coin-paid vow."
                                A. WEBSTER.

"GRACE, my dear," said her mother one day, when she thought a sufficient time had elapsed for her daughter to have considered the subject she had put before her, "your father must give Mr. O'Brien some answer to his proposal when he returns to Limerick. Have you thought over what we spoke of a day or two ago?"

"What else could I think of, mother? Such proposals don't come every day."

"No, my dear. Such brilliant prospects do not fall to every one's lot either. Your father and I, my dear, will be proud to see our daughter the mistress of Ballygany Castle."

"How do you know you will ever see me

in that exalted position, mother? The die is not cast yet."

"You are perfectly right, my dear, to take proper time to consider before deciding on such a step. But I do not contemplate that you will forget all the advantages you must gain by yielding to this proposal of Mr. O'Brien. You can have no possible objection to him personally, I think, my dear. He has a handsome, pleasing figure, and we all know his generous, benevolent disposition too well of old to doubt it for a moment."

"Yes, we have known him long enough, certainly," said Grace, with a touch of sarcasm in her tone.

"And that is a great recommendation, my dear, in my eyes. One can never know what people are in these disturbed times, unless you have known them all your life. It is all very well occasionally to make a new acquaintance, and we could not have made a more agreeable one than Captain Ward; but one needs something more to depend on for a life-long connexion. Now,

I would as soon doubt your father as Manus."

"He has had years enough, goodness knows, to sow his wild oats twice over, if he had any; but, poor old fellow, I don't believe he ever had any to sow."

"No, my dear; he was as steady in his young days as he is now."

"Was he ever young, mother? Dear me, what a dreary thing it must be never to waver from the path of duty."

"You will reap the advantage of it now, my dear. One never knows how a young man may have involved his patrimony in his youth when he has been about the world much; and your life at the castle will be such a settled, certain thing, so different from the life I led when your father and I were first married."

"A settled life? Could there be anything more unpleasant?"

"You can get him to travel, dear; there is so much moving about now-a-days, he will think nothing of it. But you can settle all these things when you meet; your father will probably bring him back with him when he returns."

"Not unless I am going to marry him, I suppose, mother?"

"Certainly not; the man must not be brought here on false pretences; but I think I may tell your father, my dear, that you see no objection to the connexion?"

"That *you* see no objection, you mean, mother; I did not think I had passed any opinion on the subject."

"Grace, dear, there can be but one opinion on the subject. I thought we had come to that conclusion before?"

"You did; I certainly did not, and it remains to be seen yet how it will all end, as far as I am concerned."

"But, my dear, your father's wishes and mine! Will they have no weight with you?"

"I will have to do the deed, and live with Manus, mother; so I think my opinion must have some more weight. You and my father will only have to look on at the play, I must take part in every scene."

"Certainly; but it will be a scene you have always looked forward to, my dear: position, wealth, ease, luxury, I may say, will be your surroundings."

"I know, mother, and they are tempting; but my mind is undecided. I never thought it would be so. I never dreamt that these things would be all I needed; now that they are within my reach, I almost fear to touch them."

"Grace, what has come over you? These notions are not your own."

"Why not, mother? Do you not know that I have always been as changeable as the wind? How came you to count so securely on my opinion?"

"It is time for you to become less uncertain in your ideas on these subjects now, Grace. You have quite too much sense, I am sure, to be carried away by a passing fancy."

"Mother, I cannot change my nature."

"But it is not your nature, my dear, to forget the advantages which a position like the one now offered to you will afford; no one knows better than yourself the value of such an opening."

"Yes; you have always put these things prominently before me; and it is certainly not your fault, mother, if I fail to take advantage of them now."

"I have always had your good too much at heart, Grace, to do otherwise, and I feel sure you will not disappoint my hopes now by any foolish hesitation."

"No one has 'my good,' as you call it, mother, more at heart, I assure you, than I have myself; so you may depend on my studying the subject attentively. I don't see what hurry there need be about it, unless indeed for poor Manus; he is right to make no delay at his time of life."

"You cannot keep the man in a state of uncertainty; it is not fair. We must consider him a little in the matter."

"If he does not choose to wait my pleasure he need not; but, mother, I cannot make up my mind in such hot haste."

"This is mere folly, Grace, and in every way unworthy of the trouble I have taken in your bringing up. Mr. O'Brien has your father's and my approbation; that alone should make your decision easy."

"If either of you will marry the man for me, perhaps it would; but you see the result of the step for good or evil will altogether fall on me."

"Grace, I never thought a child of mine could forget herself so entirely as to indulge in such impertinences, speaking of father or mother. I will hear no more from you on the subject at present; and if it does not suit you to come to a decision before your father leaves home, I will undertake myself to send a proper message by him to Mr. O'Brien: you seem in a humour just now which renders you incapable of judging for yourself in such a matter."

"Do not be too hard on the child, wife," said the Major, who, entering the room, had heard the last words. "It is but natural she should find it difficult to make up her mind."

"I do not object to that so much, Major, though it is indeed a senseless affectation on

Grace's part, but such extravagant language as she has not scrupled to use, is in my eyes unpardonable."

"It is our own fault, we have spoiled the girl. Is not that it, Grace? But you will be a good girl in the end, and allow your mother to judge what is best."

"I cannot, father; you have spoilt me. I do not know what it is not to please myself in everything."

"But what more do you want to please you in this matter, my girl? Manus is a good fellow, as you know well, and with him I am sure you may please yourself all your life long."

"I can't tell, father, how it is ; but I feel as if this marriage could never please me quite."

"Nonsense, girl! you do not know what a life you may lead at the castle. Think of that, and don't be a fool. What else would you have? You and Manus have always been the best of good friends, so it can't be that you don't like the man himself; unless, indeed, that you've got some foolish fancy in your little head, Gracie, for some one else."

"Don't put such an idea into her head, Major. Grace has been too well brought up to indulge in any mere vagaries; she will come to her senses by-and-bye, and will live to thank us in after-life for putting the right course so plainly before her."

Grace did not answer, but her lip curled with something like derision at her mother's self-satisfied words, and then the expression of her face assumed a cold look of resistance —obstinacy it might almost be termed.

CHAPTER XLVII.

"Ah! should'st thou live but once love's sweets to prove,
Thou wilt not love to live, unless thou live to love."
SPENSER.

THE Major returned to head-quarters with but little satisfaction for his friend Manus. Grace was obdurate: neither her mother's bitterness nor her father's milder arguments could prevail upon her to come to any decision on the subject. Their anxiety to further Mr. O'Brien's cause seemed to have stimulated her to a resistance she scarcely understood herself; but as each day passed a stronger barrier seemed to rise up in her imagination against the plan, and its advantages, which she could acknowledge readily enough at times, grew less vivid under the workings of another influence which till now she boasted herself proof against. It was the evening of the day her father had left, and escaping from a rather stormy interview with her mother, who could not refrain from expressing her dissatisfaction in bitter taunts, Grace wandered up and down under the trees, vexed and moody. Why had this sudden change come over her? Why could she not enter into all her mother's plans with the satisfaction which a few weeks before would have been the natural course of events? Could she care so much already for him who had walked on this same path with her a short time before? She longed to see him once again, to test her feelings in his presence, and again and again she assured herself she would be able to dispel the fancy, and turn her thoughts to the more substantial good which lay at her feet. Pausing in her walk, she leant against a tree, and looked away across the landscape, lit up by the declining autumn sun, which cast long waving shadows over the green, undulating fields stretching far and wide around. But one object was to be seen moving, and on it she fixed her eyes. It was a solitary horseman quickly making his way across the country, without heed of road or byway. Grace watched curiously for some time, and then, as the rider drew rein, it seemed as if she must know the tall figure and its easy, careless bearing. Were her wishes to be so quickly fulfilled? Would she see him so soon again? And would her whim vanish in his bodily presence as quickly as it seemed to have sprung up?

The rider sees her now; and, turning his horse with a sudden motion, Captain Ward —for it is he—is soon at her side.

"What fortunate thought brought you out here this evening? Did my good angel tell you I was coming, Miss Colthurst?" he asked, jumping from his saddle.

"The evening was fine and the house lonely: my father left us to-day," said Grace, more confused than she had ever felt in her life.

"Then I must thank the evening and your father's absence for this pleasant meeting."

"You were coming to the house, were you not?"

"I was coming to see you; and I almost feared to intrude on your mother's hospitality so soon again, so nothing could have suited me better than to meet you here."

"How did you get away so soon again?" she said, in an effort to say something.

"Oh, I can always manage such things. Nothing would have kept me from seeing you, Miss Colthurst. I want to learn from your own lips what your fate is to be."

"My fate? what do you know about it?" It seemed as if he must have been reading her thoughts.

"I know," he said—with a laugh which grated upon her ear, though she could not explain why—"I know everything. I know they want you to marry that old fool O'Brien, and I have come this evening to hear the story from yourself—to hear whether you have, like all the rest, his pounds, shillings and pence learnt off by heart, and his broad acres measured to an inch."

"I cannot understand how you could

have heard anything of this, Captain Ward."

"Did I not tell you I knew everything?" he said, excited for a moment out of his usual quiet, almost indifferent tone. "My authority could not be better. Your brother took care to let me into the secret; but perhaps we may outwit them yet."

"What do you mean, Captain Ward?" said Grace, raising her eyes shyly to his.

"I will tell you what I mean, Grace. Don't turn away; help me with your eyes to speak the truth. They want to sacrifice you, to sell you, because of his wealth, his position; and he will buy you because you are young and beautiful, because you will make his dreary old ruin of a castle less wretched, and his mouldy old life less stagnant. None of them care to think what it will be to you: none of them consider what the sacrifice must be to you. But I know how you will pine away your life watching that old man hobbling into his grave, and how your beauty and your youth will fade away, shut up in the dreary, tumbledown old ruin."

"What else can I do?" she said, humbly, her usual light manner sobered by the fascination of his earnestness.

"You can tell them you will not be sold —that you have a heart to feel as other people, and a spirit, bolder and stronger than many another, that are not to be bartered away."

"But have I a heart? Do I care, do you think? Sometimes I think it does not matter. I like money, and the comforts that money can buy. Perhaps they are right; I will not feel the sacrifice?"

"Will you not?" he said, almost with derision. "But I tell you you will; to the day of your death it will be a chain binding you down. You will never be free. You will never know what it is to live—to live as I would have you live, with all your heart and soul."

"You are mistaken in me, Captain Ward. You do not know that by this sacrifice, as you call it, I will gain what I have always looked forward to as the very summit of life and happiness."

"Looked forward to! Perhaps so; but now that the time has come, how is it? Can you look forward now to the long days and years with him? Tell me, Grace, —tell me truly,—will his money and his good things satisfy you now?"

"Why should they not?" she said, almost inaudibly.

"Because I can give you more, and you can give me all I need. Is it not so, Grace; can we not satisfy each other?"

"I do not know: sometimes I feel as if I wanted so much."

"Nothing that I cannot give you, Grace. You thought you could do without love, that it was a folly you could never know; but I tell you you cannot—you love me, Grace, though you will not own it to yourself. I know you better than you do yourself, and you must not, you cannot deny it."

She could not, proud and self-willed as she was, she could not if she would put the truth of his words away from her. Silently she listened as he told her what she was to him, and what their life together would be.

"It must be, you see it must be; if we want to know what life is, we must live it together, and I can give you all you have looked forward to. Trust me and you shall never know what want is; nay, more, you shall have all the luxuries, all the comforts that O'Brien could have heaped upon you."

"But what will they say? You do not know what a strong will my mother has."

"She may have, but we need not test it: your father has a soft heart, he will forgive you when it is past remedy."

"What do you mean?" she said, with a start.

"I mean that we will carry out this little plan of ours with as little trouble as possible. It is no use annoying ourselves and them with a wordy war; we must take the reins into our own hands, and once the race is fairly started, they must let us run it out as we please. Leave all to me; I will manage it all, and I will not ask you again to trust me, for you cannot help it; you must do it in spite of yourself."

"Am I to do nothing, then; are you strong enough to bear all the burden?"

"Have I not been pretty strong already to have gone as far as I have to-day successfully? It was my strong will brought you out here this evening, and made you listen while I told you what you needed, and this strength will give you all you want yet, and overcome all obstacles if you only trust in it. But tell me what are the obstacles? Your mother was not unfavourable to me before this O'Brien appeal came on: who knows but she may be won over yet, and, as I said before, your father at least would not stand out if the deed were done."

"I fear my mother has made up her mind to this match with Manus; but come in now, and I will leave you to work your own way."

"Yes, but before we go, give me some comfort; tell me in your own words what I have told you; strong as I am, I am only strong in the love you can give me."

And so Grace Colthurst was won, the vision was a reality now; the influence which had stolen so unconsciously over her was a living power and will from which there was no escape.

CHAPTER XLVIII.

"From life without freedom, ah who would not fly?
For one day of freedom, oh who would not die?
* * * * * *
And oh, e'en if freedom from this world be driven,
Despair not—at least we shall find her in Heaven."
MOORE.

ALL-POWERFUL as Captain Ward had proved himself with Grace, he was not so with her mother. His fascination of manner and undaunted assurance could not conquer her determination that Grace should marry Manus, whose substantial reality of position was too apparent to admit of a doubt; and, irritated by the unlooked-for opposition from Grace to his proposal, she assumed an impenetrable front of cold disdain to meet all Captain Ward's fair-sounding arguments in favour of his suit.

"I will try what I can do with your father, Grace," he said, when the time came for him to go next morning.

"Mother is the strongest; she will never let it be," said Grace, sadly.

"Never! I will see to that; be ready, Grace, for me; trust me and their opposition matters not."

And then he was gone, and Grace stood watching him as he rode hastily away. She could hardly believe the change that had come over her, so suddenly it seemed. But there was no uncertainty, no wavering in her mind now; her mother's bitter scornful words had finished the work which the outspoken assurance of Captain Ward had begun. He had told her that she loved him, and she knew it now without a doubt: he was right, life with him would be life indeed, and a union with Manus a bondage unendurable to both.

"Isma, could you not speak to my mother? she might hear reason from you," she said, as her cousin joined her.

"I have spoken, but she said I knew nothing about it; that it was impossible for me to judge."

"But she is wrong; you do know how it

is, you know that it is a question of happiness or misery to me."

"I think I do: but, Grace, dear, you must have patience with aunt; you know you thought almost as she did a short while ago; you are changed, and she is the same; she cannot understand how it is with you."

"Yes, I am changed, and I never dreamt it would be in this way; but I cannot help it, that is all; you could not help it were you in my place, could you, child?"

"I don't know, Grace, we are so different —so different in every way."

"But you do know what it is to love. You are so cunning, Isma, you would never tell anything about yourself, but I know very well there is some one no person could induce you to give up, if you were told to do so as I am."

"They will give in. Aunt could not oppose you long; only wait quietly, and it will come round all right as you wish."

"I will not wait quietly as you say. Why should I? I hate waiting, and they have taught me to please myself too long, to allow me to sacrifice myself for a whim of theirs now."

"Oh, Grace, do not do anything hastily. Promise me you wont. You will be sorry all your life long, if you displease them. Think how they love you—how you are all in all to them."

"I will promise nothing. You are a little fool, Isma. If they love me, why should they prevent me from pleasing myself?"

"They are anxious to do what they think best for you, I am sure. Trust them, and wait a little."

"Think best! How do they know what is best? Will you let them choose for you, little Isma, when the time comes, eh? I think not; it is easy to preach patience till then."

"Perhaps so. It is hard to judge for another, but I have great faith in waiting."

"That is the reason you are so quiet and patient now, but what is *he* waiting for, I wonder? The war is over, and still your wild Irishman is not forthcoming. What will you do if he never come?"

"I suppose I must only wait on," said Isma, with a quiet smile.

"Ah! you have actually acknowledged his existence at last, child. Well, I wish you joy of your waiting: it is dreary work, particularly when one has to listen to mother's pleasant sarcasms. I hope they may never fall on your head; if so, 1 defy you to wait. Nothing is too dreadful to contemplate which would free one from their stinging power."

It was the morning of the sixth of October; the Irish regiments in Limerick were assembled in their several quarters, and the look of excitement and interest on all faces told of some unusual work on hand. The coming day must decide the fate of many. To go, or to stay? was the anxious question which puzzled the hearts of the men listening, some with a hopeless, careless, expression on their pale, tired faces, others with a dogged look of already fixed determination which no arguments could alter, while their chiefs exhorted them to follow their lead, to leave their country for a time—to return in triumph on some not far distant day. As a last expedient to fix their wavering decision, Sarsfield had caused their spiritual advisers to exert their eloquence on the patriotic side, and at this moment he stood pale and haggard with emotion, while the clear voice of the chaplain of his regiment rang out in earnest pleading.

"Soldiers!" he said, "listen to your sentence, your doom. Listen to the words of the Lord, great and terrible in judgment. 'Lo!' he says, 'I will make thee small among the heathen, and despised among men,' and wherefore, my brethren, is it so? Wherefore will the Lord our God forget His love and His tender pity for us, the children of His church, the helpless sheep of His pasture? Is it because in the fortunes of war we have failed, because strength and victory are in the hands of our enemies, and we are weak and humbled before their faces? No—the Lord is righteous in His thoughts and clear when he judges. He will not willingly afflict or grieve the children of men. To cleanse us and to purify us from the dross of the world He has brought this evil upon us, and it is for us to bow before Him in silent submission, and in His own good time He will raise us up again, and lay low our enemies in the dust. But, soldiers and fellow-countrymen, if we turn aside from Him now, if we follow false gods, false teachers, false prophets, behold I say unto you in His name this day, that the curse will fall upon you and your children from generation to generation, even for ever. He will make you small among the heathen, and utterly despised among men. Come out from among them, I say, and be ye separated from the workers of iniquity, from the blasphemers of our Church, from the forsakers of our holy religion. They will hem you in on every side, they will encroach upon your landmarks, they will take from you your birthright—the birthright of your fathers—the birthright of your sons and your daughters. Around your hearthstones others shall sit. Under the shadow of your trees your enemies shall shelter. And you! where will you be, oh my brothers? The prophet tells us you will be small, yea, small and despised, of no reputation, forgotten, dead. The religion of your forefathers will be heard no more: the voice of your Church will be silent in the land. Your priests will no more bless your children, no more bless your hands joined in sacred wedlock, or cold and stiff as they lie crossed on your breasts when your eyes are closed in the last long sleep of death. Never again will your brave men go forth to conquer. Never again will the standard of your King and your country float unfettered in the breeze. Men of might there will be in the land. Another standard will be unfurled on your hill-tops. Another King and another Church will rule your country; but you will be small, despised among men. Must it be so? Will you sit down, my brethren, under the yoke? Will you bow your heads in the dust at the feet of your enemies? Will you wait and see the degradation that will fall upon you? Or will you remember this day that you are Irish soldiers with your country's weal in your hands, either to cast away uncared for and rejected, or to cherish and nourish till this calamity is overpast, and our day of hope once more has dawned. You crave for peace and rest. Yes, I see it in your faces, and the conquerors will not withhold it from you, they tell you, with their fair words and smiling faces. Beware of them ! Beware of them, my children. They come to you as wolves in sheep's clothing. Heed them not. Hearken not to their soft words. Hear me, your father in the Lord. Follow your countrymen who have led you in the path of duty till this day. Follow them, the true followers of the Church. Follow them, I say. Be guided by them, even though you cannot see your way, even though you must needs leave your fatherland, your wives, and your little ones. Trust them. Go with them, and they will lead you back, to hurl down the standard of the usurper, to avenge the blood of your countrymen, and to vindicate the smitten Church of your faith. Small and despised you shall not be in that day. The Lord himself will fight for you. He will revenge His own elect. He will fight for his people. Your Redeemer is strong. The Lord of Hosts is his name. He will thoroughly plead your cause, that He may give rest to the land. You must choose this day, my brethren, whom ye will serve. Be not deceived, I tell you. 'God is not mocked; whatsoever a man soweth that shall he also reap.' Peace you want; believe me, it is not for traitors: it is for you, Irishmen; only be true. Forsake not your leaders in the cause, and your peace is sure. It is before you, look not behind, follow on, press forwards, sit not down, blinded, deceived, vanquished. 'Make bright your arrows, gather your shields. The Lord hath raised up the spirit of the Kings to help us yet again.' Once more the standard shall be set up, the temple of the Lord established, and the rest, the peace shall be ours for ever."

He ceased. The last effort had been made, the moment for decision had nearly come, and Sarsfield saw the garrison file out from the town to take their place in the vast meadow on the banks of the Shannon, with mingled feelings of doubt and hope. He could do no more: each man must take the final step for himself, and whether for good or for evil, who could tell?

The troops, about fourteen thousand infantry, were drawn up on the large open space on the banks of the river. A strange forlorn appearance they presented after the months of hardship and privation they had undergone. Ragged, clamorous, and undisciplined, a spectator might have thought it could matter but little whether they stayed or went: but Sarsfield, who knew better, perhaps, than any one present what the Irish could do, pictured to himself the order, spirit, and energy which a few months' training, with proper food and clothing, might create out of the unpromising materials before him. Nor were the English leaders blind to the dangers of augmenting and strengthening their French neighbours with the best blood of Ireland, which, if left in the country, would in time settle down, assimilated with the conquering race in common interest. With almost as keen an enthusiasm they went through the ranks of the Irish, exhorting, explaining, and urging all the advantages to themselves and their country they would gain by throwing their fortunes in with King William, taking service in his ranks, or returning in peace to their homes. Copies of the proclamation promising protection and restoration to all who would stay in the country were scattered about, and every expedient was taken to impress the minds of the people with the ruin which would fall upon them in a foreign land.

Grave, anxious faces were to be seen on both sides; the French officers alone seemed to have any inclination to treat the decision with levity.

The grotesque, uncouth appearance of the troops could not escape their derision, and they commented freely on the impression the Irish soldiers would make on French minds.

"Lucan is a brave man to face the

reception of such an importation to France," said D'Usson to some of his companions as they rode slowly through the ranks. "He had better furnish them with war paint and feathers to complete the picture."

"Ah! he sees more in these fellows than we do, I suspect," replied one of his countrymen.

"We are blind, I presume he would insinuate, to their virtues and the advantages of light clothing. For my part I marvel what our Parisian friends will say to their style: shoes and stockings, you see, for the most part are forgotten in their costumes. They are prepared, my friend, for a race, and but one garment would seem to be the regulation; and that, too, in scant measure. The economy and simplicity displayed in their attire are in truth worthy of remark: how terrible will be the contrast between their unsophisticated appearance and the elaborate extravagance of our troops in la belle France! Lucan," he said as he drew near the General, "have you seriously considered the shock our friend Louis will experience when you present to him your Irish regiments in full dress?"

"My only idea at present, D'Usson, is to secure the regiments themselves, and, to tell the truth, I am not afraid of the ultimate result: there is stuff enough in these poor fellows to compensate for any outward defects."

" You are right, certainly, to leave no superfluous bone and sinew to the mercy of those cold-blooded English fellows. Let them stand on their own legs, if they will, and it is plain they dread the position. See how stern and important our friend the Baron Ginkel looks; he is almost as much in earnest as yourself, General."

" Yes, he has the sense to understand that Ireland without the Irish is not the country he bargained for. They will need some of the enthusiasm of our nature to keep things going here. Besides, England cannot afford to maintain a perpetual garrison, this side of the water, which they must do if they have the fear of an invasion from France before their eyes, and they are sharp enough to know that we do not mean to take the burden of these troops upon us without some ulterior object."

"How will it be, think you, General? Are these Irish inclined to follow our fortunes, or to take advantage of the terms offered to them in this country?"

"I can hardly judge. But see, the time has come now! We shall all know soon enough how it will be. God grant that my efforts may not have been in vain!"

The troops advanced as arranged previously to pass in review. All who had determined to remain in Ireland were ordered to file off at a particular point, while those who declared for France passed on without a break.

First in order came the Royal regiment, fourteen hundred strong. Almost breathlessly Sarsfield watched them near the fatal spot. Would they turn aside, or would they pass on to where he stood? Steadily they came on and passed—passed all but seven. A loud cheer rose from the Irish side, and their hopes rose. But on came the next regiment, chiefly Ulster men. Among their number we may recognise some old friends. Surely we know the ambling gait of that foremost gaunt steed ; he will not be kept back; first he must be, come what will. It is Louis le Grand and Sir Teague. Poor Louis' sides are not much better covered than in the Sligo days, and his legs look longer and more forlorn than ever; but his spirit is fresh and buoyant still, and he and his master seem to be as satisfied to be seen and admired as of old. On they come as gaily as ever, Sir Teague pleased and proud to find himself as usual the centre of observation.

"So-ho! Louis, old fellow, quietly now," he remonstrated as the animal plunged and snorted impatient of restraint. "We must do the thing with a dignity befitting the occasion, Louis. I have explained matters to you before, Louis—a soldier must give in to his fate. Quietly, quietly, old fellow: we cannot alter our destiny!" he said with a struggle as a sudden jerk from Louis almost unseated his master, leaving his wig and white beaver unbecomingly awry. All eyes were turned on the curious spectacle as Sir Teague and Louis approached the turning point, and Sir Teague's voice could be heard in explanation to his refractory horse. " Nerve yourself to the point, Louis, my old fellow—soldiers must submit. You and I are too old for foreign travel; this way, Louis—we'll lay our old bones in the old country, God bless her! What more could soldiers do than we have done for her? Now, Louis, the turn must be made." But Louis thought differently, it was apparent. Indignant at the efforts of his master to turn him towards the English side, he plunged violently with a snort of defiance, shook himself free from his rider, and galloped on in triumph to the Irish goal. Sir Teague, considerably dishevelled, slowly gathered himself up, philosophically consoling himself for the disaster with reflections on Louis' peculiarities. " Ah, the poor fellow ! No one but himself could have done it, true and loyal to the last—but mistaken in his judgment; carried away by impulse—a trick I could never break him of, the greatest fault a soldier could commit."

"How is this, Sir Teague?" said Colonel Scott, who was not far off. "You have parted company with Louis after all."

"Ah, Colonel, is that you? You are surprised to see me in this situation, no doubt, but you know of old the obstinacy of poor Louis' disposition. I assure you I explained the whole matter to him, and the expediency of our taking this turn, but he would not listen to reason, and guided by his fiery spirit, which long years of discipline have failed to tame, he has taken his own course, and left me to follow the path my calm judgment saw was the proper one for both him and me to pursue. You will understand, Colonel, what my motives are, though poor Louis has been deaf to my arguments in the matter."

"I have no doubt, Sir Teague, you have carefully weighed the subject, and you will find many others of the same opinion."

"You see, Colonel, ten or twenty years ago, Louis and I might have safely taken a different course, but neither he nor I are as young as we used to be, though to tell you the truth, Colonel, I don't think any one would know it; but one must be cautious, and consider the future, as I have always tried to impress upon my subordinates, and as I dare say you remember of old, Colonel."

"You are perfectly justified in your choice, I have no doubt, Sir Teague, but I must pass on. You have plenty of companions in this regiment, I fear; the Ulster men are not half Irish in their sympathies."

He was right, and it was Ginkel's turn to show satisfaction this time. In the succeeding regiments there was much diversity of opinion, but when the trial was over, the result was found to be that a majority had declared for France.

CHAPTER XLIX.

" Oh how bitter a thing it is to look into happiness through another man's eyes."—SHAKSPEARE.

"I NEED scarcely ask you if you are satisfied with the day's work, Lord Lucan," said Major Colthurst, as the officers conversed in groups, after the review was over.

"I am pretty well assured, I think, Major, that I need not go into exile alone: you see we are jealous of leaving you any of our good comrades on this side the water."

"Yes, and you have succeeded in your desire better than I expected. I imagined you would have found those wretched fellows harder to move."

"They have not much to stay for, I think, Major. They have not much faith in your good intentions yet, however it may be by-and-bye."

"I don't think we grudge the majority of them to you, Lord Lucan, unless it had been in our power to induce you and some of your officers to throw in your lot with us into the bargain."

"I can assure you at least of one titled officer, Major Colthurst," said Colonel Scott. "Our old Sligo governor took the fatal turn to-day."

"Sir Teague! By Jove, did he?" said Colonel Mitchelburne. "It would be a curious study to investigate how many masters the same Sir Teague has served under in his time, he and his famous charger, Louis le Grand!"

"Ah! poor Louis has deserted him at the last: he followed our fortunes nobly, and left Sir Teague in rather an undignified position at the turning point."

"What a blow to the poor knight."

"Not at all, Mitchelburne. I assure you he justified his own and the animal's conduct in the most comfortable manner, as proud of Louis' spirit as of his own judgment and foresight; he was by no means abashed."

"And I don't find fault with the old fellow either," said Mitchelburne. "He served you faithfully while he was about it, and he is free to do the same by us now."

"Certainly," said Major Colthurst, "the old fellow has a right to use his sense when he has any, and you had better take a lesson, too, from him, Colonel Scott."

"The die is cast for me, Major; I am afraid I cannot boast any of my friend Sir Teague's good sense in such a matter."

"Then you leave Ireland, Colonel, with the rest."

"Such is my intention, Major."

"You must excuse me for questioning you, Colonel, but you are aware that the little girl, Isma O'Neil, is my niece, and I promised her to learn somewhat as to your future plans."

They had moved aside from the other officers, and the Colonel answered quickly,

"I have been anxious to speak to you before this on the subject, Major Colthurst, but my time has been so fully occupied since the siege was raised."

"No doubt, Colonel; but the best plan will be for you to accompany me home, and see your little friend for yourself; she will hardly forgive you, I think, if you leave the country without a word with her."

"You are very kind, Major Colthurst; but my time is scarcely my own even now. Our departure for France will be hurried."

"What shall I say to the child, then, Colonel? She will not take this desertion on your part kindly, I think."

"Poor child!" said Scott, tenderly. "I think, if you will allow me, Major, I can substitute another visitor who will more than make up to her for my absence. My brother—I think you have met him—Lieutenant Scott; he stays in this country by my especial desire, that our father's name should not be forgotten, and, as Miss O'Neil's natural guardian is her uncle, I beg you will consider my brother's claims to her hand. They are both young—almost too young to think of such things, but circumstances threw them together, and I believe them to be sincerely attached to each other."

In measured, constrained tones he spoke, and no one could have guessed the effort such words cost him to utter. Pleading for his brother—why not for himself? Was Conn's love for her stronger, fresher? Had the intensity of his own passion died away? Had it only been the spark of a moment? No, Conn could not, in all the buoyancy of his youth, feel a more earnest love for her than Edward Scott now felt, even as he spoke. As intense and absorbing as ever was the feeling, and it needed all the unselfish strength of his nature to put his passion aside.

"Ah! is this the way it is?" said the Major, turning a searching glance at his companion. "I had somehow got a different notion into my head—an absurd one, too. To be sure, you could be the girl's father almost. Young people will like young people to the end of time, and I suppose it's natural; but it's awkward sometimes, you see."

"Awkward, did you say, Major? Perhaps you will oblige me by stating your objections to this connexion. My brother will have our small family property in the North, and I can assure you Miss O'Neil could not find one more worthy of her than my brother Conn."

"Probably not, Colonel; you mistake me, I think. I do not see what objections there can be to the match. I only mentioned that awkward things will occur sometimes, you know, in such cases. As to your brother, I have no reason to cast a doubt upon his suitability to my niece, as you tell me he settles down like a Christian in this country. He must come to Leagh, and we shall see what the ladies say; they will be sure to find out if there ought to be any hitch in the matter."

Later in the same evening, the two brothers met in Lord Lucan's quarters, and the Colonel, drawing Conn aside, told him of his interview with Major Colthurst. Radiant with pleasure, Conn heard of the prospect of the fulfilment of his wishes; and

Mary Sarsfield, watching at a distance, found herself speculating on their earnest conversation, and contrasting the expression on the brothers' faces.

Sterner and graver than ever, Edward Scott sat with compressed lips, speaking now and then in a low, quiet tone in answer to the rapid, excited speech of his brother, who poured out almost like a schoolboy his plans and hopes—his face flushed with pleasure, and his eye bright with expectation.

"Edward, why will you go? Why will you not stay and share our happiness?"

"There can be no share in such happiness: there ought not to be," said the elder brother.

"But what shall I do without you, Edward? How shall we get on without your help?"

"You will not miss me when you have her, Conn. I should only be an intruder upon your peace."

"How can you say such things, Edward? You an intruder —you, who have been a father to both of us? You were her friend long before she saw me."

"Yes; and, so God help me, I will be your friend still—yours and hers too, Conn."

"Yes, I know you will; you must bè. But why not give up these foreign plans and stay with us?"

"That is impossible, Conn: I must go, and it were better so. You will be happy, and I——"

"You must be happy too. Why have you never married, Edward? Is there no one good enough in the world for you? Why have you never found an Isma? Have you never——"

"Hush, Conn. You do not know what you are saying," was the sharp, quick answer, and then more softly he added: "Never mind me, Conn: do not trouble yourself with my affairs. Come, we have isolated ourselves long enough from our friends;" and rising, he moved across the room.

"How pleased and animated your brother looks to-night, Colonel Scott," said Mary

Sarsfield, as he drew near to where she sat, somewhat apart from the other occupants of the room, in a deep window-seat.

"Yes; it is the lad's nature, and, besides, he has bright prospects before him."

"Bright prospects in Ireland! How can that be?"

"Every one is not so unselfishly patriotic as you are, Miss Sarsfield. Many of us are quite content with a bright home circle of our own, where the troubles of our country are forgotten at least for a time."

"I suppose it must be the case: we are more influenced by our personal feelings in such things than we are at all willing to allow."

"Yes, but there are some like yourself, Miss Sarsfield, who throw their whole heart and interests into a cause, and cast off all other influences."

"We may profess to do so; but were we tried I doubt if we could prove stronger in face of a great personal sacrifice. Do you think, Colonel Scott, if you were in your brother's place, you could turn away from the quiet home life, and go with us to France as willingly as you now intend?"

"There might be a harder sacrifice even than that, I think, Miss Sarsfield. Conn might go now with a hope of return to cheer him, the thought of a true heart waiting for him, never changing through the long days of suspense. Another might go now with every hope he had known in the past blotted out, and nothing in the future to look to but a struggling and lonely existence."

"With no hope even of the country's restoration?" said the girl.

"Ay! I fear my picture was altogether a personal one, bearing out your argument that after all we have a stronger interest in ourselves than in anything else. Still I must own that the thought of our country does not add to the hopefulness."

"Will it always be so? Will there never be any hope—never any brightness for Ireland?"

"Its brightest days may be yet to come, Miss Sarsfield. You are not among the doubting ones, surely. I should not have allowed my gloomy apprehensions to trouble you."

"No, but I should have had more faith to put them to flight. I am afraid, too, I am allowing my personal feelings to influence my patriotic ones. There seems so little sometimes to trust in or to look to for help."

"Perhaps brighter days may dawn for all of us in France: at any rate we must hope so."

"Yes, but I hate a foreign place, and my coming back seems so uncertain, but you will have to come to see your brother and his wife. Are you satisfied with his choice, Colonel Scott?"

"Miss O'Neil is quite worthy of him, and I dare say you know by this time, Miss Sarsfield, what the lad is to me. But I do not look forward to seeing them again, unless the chances of war bring me to this country."

"Ah, but they will. My uncle looks to return with a considerable force in a few months."

"Your faith is coming back, I see, in spite of my gloomy forebodings."

"When I think of my uncle, I am always more hopeful. He is so strong and steadfast."

"Yes, and you generally take after him, Miss Sarsfield."

"I try to do so at least, and you must follow his example, too, Colonel Scott. My uncle has a wonderful influence over other people."

"He has, and we must leave all our dark fancies behind us when we land in France. There will be plenty of work there for us, organizing the troops, if we are to do any good in the end."

"Yes, and work is the salt of life, you know they say, Colonel Scott," she said, as she moved away with a smile of hope in her soft grey eyes.

CHAPTER L.

"Love gives esteem, and then he gives desert:
He either finds equality, or makes it:
Like Death, he knows no difference in degrees,
But planes and levels all."—DRYDEN.

A PARTY had arrived at Leagh, and a pleasant buzz of talking was to be heard in the gloomy old sitting-room, Mrs. Colthurst rejoicing in her son's company, after his lengthened absence, and Frank himself enjoying all the attentions which he never lacked at home. Grace hung over her father's chair, hearing all his news and anxious seemingly to assert her right to the caresses which as his pet and plaything were always ready for her at his side. Isma sat somewhat apart, silent, but happier perhaps than all the others, for was there not a figure in the group which was not strange to her, and a bright glance of love to meet her every look? Yes, Conn had come, come at last, and there was no need for them to ask each other had they forgotten the happy hours passed, so long ago it seemed now, in Cousin Deborah's little dark parlour, far away in Sligo? The time of separation had only drawn them nearer in thought, and strengthened the half-uttered vows between them. Mrs. Colthurst had been taken by storm, and to tell the truth had but little thought to bestow on her niece's doings just at present: Grace's far more important affair must be discussed and arranged.

"Well, Major," she began, with unusual energy, when they were alone together, "this is a pretty state of affairs. You have come home without Manus, and, as far as I can learn from you, with no more definite news from him; and here we are with Grace as obstinate as a mule, and no way made toward showing her how things must be."

" I told you before, my dear, that Manus refused to come, unless I could assure him of the reception Grace would give him, and how could I tell what line the girl would take if I had brought him here? I could not risk the man's being insulted, you know."

"Grace knows better than to do anything to offend your friend, Major, but I am at my wits' end to know what to do. Captain Ward has actually been here since. I don't know what passed between him and Grace, but I see her mind is made up since, and I thought it better to wait till you returned to urge the matter further."

"What brought the fellow Ward here? But you may set your mind at ease on that point, my dear. He will scarcely have the face to show here again. I hear there are reports of indictments gone out against him, on the part of Mitchelburne, about some cattle-driving or something of the sort. Frank knows the whole story, and he will let Grace hear it too, I'll be bound."

"Indictments! You don't mean to say so: and he had the assurance to come here with such a fair face and such fair speech! Dear me! who would have thought it?"

"It's nothing so very bad, I believe, my dear; only some wild riding about the country after cattle; but it will be a very good excuse for Grace, and Manus may ride the winning horse yet."

"Indeed, I hope so, but you have no idea how obstinate she has grown. I can't understand it, I thought she was as wise as myself on such matters."

"Never fear, wife, it will all come right enough. Manus is too good a fellow to be thrown overboard. I take it you'll have no further trouble either with the little girl Isma; she will be off your hands without much question. That young Scott has thrown in his lot at home, so there can be no objection to the match, if it pleases them."

"Dear me, how you do hurry on, Major; Isma and that young fellow you brought home this evening? What do you know about it?"

"Only that he wants to marry her, and I think there is very little doubt she is of the same mind; blind as I am, I could see that much to-night."

"And he is Irish, and a Roman Catholic; her mother's fate over again. Nonsense,

Major, it must be stopped; what did you bring him here for?"

" There was nothing else to be done, my dear; and why should you put yourself out of your way to stop the young people in their match-making. I believe the young man is desirable in every way."

"What do you say to his religion?"

" Can't be helped, my dear, and if she don't object I am sure we need not. I tell you what, Frank there will be falling in love with the girl if you don't let Scott take her off. She's a pretty little piece of goods, but I don't suppose she'd come up to your notions for him."

" Scarcely. Frank would never think of such a little penniless chit: he at least has more sense, if Grace has not."

" Well, take my advice, my dear, and let the young people manage these affairs for themselves."

" And Grace, what of her?"

" Well, you see, my dear, it is a pity of Manus, and this Ward fellow is impracticable. No; I think we must interfere a little in her affair, but cautiously, you see, my dear. I will talk to her myself, and we will see what she says to Frank's stories of her hero."

Almost in listless carelessness Grace heard the rumours her brother freely told of the charges which it was said Colonel Mitchelburne was prepared to bring forward against Captain Ward, relative to his conduct during the northern campaign. A closer observer might have seen, however, a scornful curl in the girl's delicately cut lip, and a glance of defiance in her usually soft full eyes, which told of a deeper interest and a fixed determination arguing ill for Manus's suit.

She made no response, uttered no word of retort to Frank's sarcastic banter, as he rallied his mother and herself on the discernment they had shown in the choice of their newly-made friend.

"He did not let you into the secrets of his past career, I suppose, mother? Trust Ward for that: he is one of the cleverest men in that way I ever came across. He has a fair front for every one he meets, and never fails to ingratiate himself into favour, so you need not feel that he has made greater fools of you than he has of half the world beside."

"To tell you the truth, Frank, we found him a most agreeable young man, and from all I could gather, he held a very fair position in his own country."

"Oh, I dare say. Every one knows him, and no man in Ulster would care to leave any sort of prey within the same gentleman's reach, if that is what you call a desirable position, mother. I wonder what sort of a position he will find himself in when Mitchelburne brings him to bay for one or two instances of desertion and insubordination. I say, Grace, will you go bail for him?"

Provoked to speak, with flashing eyes she answered: "I do not believe it. I don't believe your insinuations, Frank; and what is more, I will not."

Before he could reply she had left the room, and he turned for explanation to his mother.

"What has come over Grace, mother? Is she really entangled with this fellow, Ward?"

"It is altogether most unfortunate, Frank, and I do not see how I am to blame in the matter, though I know you and your father will say I might have prevented it."

"Prevented what, mother? You don't mean to say there is anything serious in this flirtation."

"I don't know how it is, Frank; he has got some unaccountable influence over Grace, I am afraid. She has changed so wonderfully lately, there is no getting any good of her, and I cannot even find out how matters stand between them."

"Nonsense, mother, there must be nothing between them. What have you been about to let such an idea arise? My father seemed to have no doubt but that Manus was to be the man, and I am sure I don't see what better match she could make."

"I am quite of the same opinion, Frank, and I have done all I can to persuade Grace to set the matter at rest by a decision which of course must be come to in the end. Your father must take the matter into his own hands, and speak seriously to her. Girls will have these notions; but there will be no real difficulty in the way. When this little excitement about Captain Ward has cooled down, Grace will forget all about him, and settle her mind to more practical matters."

"I'm sure I hope so, mother. I always thought you and Grace were of one mind on such topics, and I should think you would have far more influence over her than my father; she can turn him round her finger."

"Not in this affair, I think, Frank dear. I have taken care to impress the importance of it on his mind."

"I hope it is not a case of shutting the stable-door when the steed is gone, then; for I never saw such a flash in Grace's eyes before, whatever it meant."

CHAPTER LI.

*" Whate'er befals, your life shall be my care:
One death, or one deliverance we wil share.*
                              DRYDEN.

ANGRY and excited, Grace went from the room, and hurrying down the long passage, which was darkening in the early twilight, she met her cousin's maid, Winny.

"Miss Colthurst," said the girl in a whisper, "I was to tell you to go to the beech-walk: he said he would trust me because I was Irish, and well he may, for it's us that has the weakness for such things, the Lord knows!"

"Who! what?" said Grace, bewildered.

"Now don't ye take heed to any questions of that sort, miss dear. Half a word is enough for you, leastways for the likes o' us Irish, and you are as cute as the best of us, the Lord bless you. Take your ways, natural-like, to the beech-walk, where ye've walked before now with him already, and I'll take care to tell the curious folks about that you're in your own bit of a room taking a nap."

Wrapped in her large cloak, the hood pulled closely over her face, Grace sped out to the beech-walk. Here at least no bitter taunt would meet her, no scornful word or look bring the angry light to her eyes. Slowly pacing up and down, she found Captain Ward—a shadow on his handsome features, and a weary ring in his usually gay, pleasant voice, as he greeted her.

" How can I thank you for coming, Grace, coming to see the last of me?"

" The last, not that," she said almost in a whisper.

" Yes, the last. Listen, Grace! We must be separated for ever, they will have you to go their way, to marry another, to forget me—we shall never again meet. I will never feel your hand in mine again. I will never look into your beautiful eyes for the love I know is there. You will look up to another;

but you cannot give him the same light, that is mine—mine for ever. Though I shall not see it, it is mine—mine only, and you can never give it to another, and you dare not!"

She did not answer and he went on. "It is the last time—the last time we shall ever meet; do you understand, Grace, do you understand? I know you care, you cannot help it. You care as I care, and God knows what that is: but do you understand, Grace, that in all the long days and years to come we shall never be together again?"

"I don't understand," she said passionately. "It must not be; we will, we must meet again, I care not what they say."

"Do you not care for their scorn, for their contempt? Have they not told you the world's opinion of what I am, of the disgrace they would bring upon me?"

"I do not believe it, and I have told them so."

"Do you believe, then, in my honour still, my honour that others speak so lightly of?

Grace, look up, if only once again, and tell me you believe in me, and we need not part: why should our lives be made a misery for their fancy?"

" You are true to me, at any rate," she said, looking up into his eyes restless with passion. " Why need it matter to us what the world thinks or says?"

" You are right, Grace. Why did I not know that you would believe in me, that in spite of them we shall be strong together, —together for ever, Grace, you and I. We will defy their hard words and cruel looks —you and I, Grace, together. Ah! why was I such a fool to fear that it could be otherwise?"

" But how can it be? I see in their faces they will never yield?"

" We will not ask them to yield, but they will. They will in the end, Grace, when there is no help for it. When you are mine, beyond their power to change, they will forget their hard speeches, and you will be to them what you ever were, and you don't know what you will be to me, Grace. The world says hard things of me now, perhaps I have been foolish: but together we will live it down. Your father has influence—power; he will help us; he could not forsake you, the light of his eyes, his daughter."

"I do not know. My mother is hard, you do not know how hard, and what is it that is wrong? What do they say against you?"

"You are not beginning to doubt me now, after all? But I will tell you what they say, and your father knows well what it is. He has transgressed in the same way as much, if not more than I ever did: it is nothing but what hundreds of others have done and not suffered for. You believe in me, that is enough; and why should you not, when you love me: there is no doubt, no misgiving in love, is there?"

"I suppose there ought not to be; but I must go, I shall be missed."

"You must not go till you have promised, Grace. If you go now, we may never have the same opportunity—we may never then meet again after all. There is no time to be lost, now or never, you must decide: will you trust me? Will you go with me when the time comes, when there is no other course to be taken, when, if we do not make the venture, the chance will be lost—lost for ever, Grace? Trust me, and we shall never part; be ready when I come for you. Do not hesitate, remember there will be but one alternative, a life of hopeless, dreary misery—never meeting, never seeing each other, and a life of peace, contentment, love together. Do you understand now, will you be ready, ready to fly with me, away from all the harsh censure and the bitter sarcasms?"

"You know I will. I cannot help it," she said in a voice which few would have recognised as belonging to the cold, proud Grace Colthurst.

CHAPTER LII.

"He who stems a stream with sand,
And fetters flame with flaxen band,
Has yet a harder task to prove—
By firm resolve to conquer Love!"—Scott.

"And so you have not forgotten me, Isma—not forgotten me all these long days since we used to meet so often in Cousin Deborah's little room?"

"No, Conn, I said I would not," said Isma, simply.

"And were you sure that I would not forget? Did you think we should meet again?"

"Sometimes I thought we must; that it could not be otherwise, and then when the days were slow in going over, it seemed as if I should never hear of any of you again."

"My poor little Isma, you have been lonely, but all the doubting is over now. You have had enough of it, have you not?

And you will come home to me for ever, before Edward goes. You do not know how I shall miss him—what he has always been to me."

"I think I can understand," said Isma, quietly. "I know how kind and good your brother is."

"Yes, of course you do; and I told him you would wish him to stay too, to live with us, but he will not. Nothing will persuade him from his purpose to leave the country."

"He would not be happy at home perhaps," said Isma; "after the active life he has led. It is better for him, most likely, to go away."

"Better for him? How can you think that, Isma? he was always so quiet, so fond of home—and we want him too, to make our life complete. Perhaps he would come back if you asked him. You will see him before he goes, you and I together, Isma, and then we will go down to the old place again and see Cousin Deborah, and she may lecture me as long as she likes now. Perhaps it may help to make me more worthy of you, Isma, and you will ask Edward to come back, wont you? Tell him we cannot do without his fatherly counsel."

"I do not know that I can do that, Conn. He knows that he will be more than welcome to us, and he will come if it is best for him."

"Best for him? What could be worse for him than wandering about hopelessly in a foreign land? But you have not said one word, Isma, to help to settle our plans. What does your aunt say to me? Will there be any obstacles in that quarter, think you?"

"If you only knew all the objections she has found to you already, Conn, you would not be so sanguine."

"Nonsense! What are the old dame's notions on the subject? Tell me, and I'll combat them one and all at once."

"In the first place, you know, you are Irish."

"So are you, young lady, and your father before you. Is there any objection to birds of a feather flocking together? What more says the old lady?"

"That we are not of the same faith."

"Are we not? Little she or any one else knows about that same matter. How can she tell what my faith is, or yours either?"

"You are certainly a Roman Catholic, and I a Protestant. She knows that much, Conn."

"Yes, and much good may it do her; but I tell you, Isma, it will do us no harm."

"I don't know that, Conn. It is a misfortune that it should be so."

"Do you think so, Isma? But what can be done? It is a fate we cannot alter."

"No, unless my aunt makes it a point that it shall be a barrier between us. What shall we do then, Conn?"

"Overlook the barrier, that is all. The Major would not tolerate such bigotry, I take it. After all, Isma, there is not that difference in our faith the world would make out, and we can tolerate each other as far as the difference goes, can we not, Isma?"

"I think we can. We must try, at any rate, Conn."

"Yes, leave the old lady to my tender

mercies, and I will talk her over into a proper state of amiability. I must take you to see Edward before he goes; he said he would like to see us together before he sailed."

"Did he say that?"

"Yes. So, you see, to please him it must be done; and you will put up with the wild Irish rebel, religion and all, with a pretty good grace, in spite of the old lady's notions on the subject, wont you?"

A ready smile was her only answer, and full of hopes and plans they talked over their coming prospects as only the young and happy can do.

"Isma, child, I envy you," said Grace, looking at her cousin's contented quiet face. It seemed almost as if the two girls had changed natures in the last few days. Isma's sad anxious expression had so entirely given place to one of rest and quiet pleasure, while Grace, restless and excited, was troubled and ill at ease, in strange contrast to the easy-going, immovable temperament which had been hers before.

"Why should you envy me, Grace? May

you not be as happy as I am after all? What is wrong with you, cousin? You are not happy, I see it in your face."

"Happy! no, not quite, Isma. Do you not know that they intend to make me marry whether I will or not."

"Mr. O'Brien?" said Isma.

"Yes, he is to be the happy, or rather unhappy individual."

"But it is not to be, if you decidedly object. I thought, Grace, you did not care much."

"Care! oh, no, why should I care? You care very much for Conn, don't you, child? But I am to care for no one. Ah, yes, that is the way, to be sure."

"It is only what you have always said yourself, Grace. But some one calls you, I think. Listen!"

"Yes, it is my father, I dare say. The struggle has come now, I suppose. Isma, whatever comes of it, I cannot help it: will you believe that, and pity me?"

"Yes, Grace; but if I could only help you."

"You cannot, no one could; you must only leave me to my fate."

"Grace," said her father, when she joined him, "I cannot have any more time lost about sending an answer to my good friend Manus. Your mother and I have decided that, as there is no reasonable objection on your part, we cannot do better than accept his generous offer unhesitatingly: this is the letter I have written, you can read what I have said to him."

"Father!" said Grace, pale with astonishment at so unexpected an announcement. "Stop, you must not; it cannot be."

"Must not, Grace; are you at liberty to dictate to your father?" said her mother, sternly.

"Father, listen to me," said Grace, scarcely heeding her mother's reproof. "You will not make me wretched and miserable for life. I cannot marry him, I cannot."

"You are a foolish girl, Grace. You do not know what you are saying; you are not a fit judge of what will make you happy or miserable. Trust me, my girl, and I promise you Manus will be the best husband you could find in all the country round. Why, child, you have known him all your life, you know how good and generous he is. I can't conceive what notion this is you have taken up; why on earth should there be 'a cannot' about it at all? Your mother, there, is perfectly satisfied and happy in the prospect, and she has no wish to make you either wretched or miserable."

"Grace knows very well, my dear, what my wishes and opinion on the subject are, and I take it that this burst of passion on her part is most unnecessary and unseemly. What have we, her father and mother, done to forfeit the confidence she has always placed in us?"

"Yes, Grace, that is just what I say. Trust in our good faith, and you will find we have done the best we could for you, after all."

"Father, I cannot."

"Cannot trust in your father, Grace, what next?" said her mother, indignantly.

"It seems to me that the world must be going round the wrong way, when children can say such things of their parents."

"Mother, you are cruel: you do not know how it is."

"I know very well, Grace, and I am sorry for you, that you should be so blinded to your own interests. Do you think Captain Ward will be able to give you what Mr. O'Brien will? You are sadly mistaken, my dear, if you think so, and I know you are not the girl to enjoy a life of hardship and struggle."

"Nonsense, wife; what is this you say about Ward? Grace is not dreaming of him, surely; tell her, Grace, that you are not such a fool as all that."

"I cannot; I know I am a fool, but, father, I cannot help it."

"Tush, girl, you don't know what you're doing. Ward! why, child, the fellow is only outside the prison walls on sufferance."

"What has he done, father? You cannot answer that, for you know you have done the same yourself; he told me so?"

"He did, the scoundrel! Cool, certainly. Grace, we have had enough of this; you don't know what you are saying, as I told you before, or you would scarcely venture to repeat the fellow's lies to me. Once for all, hear me: you may marry Manus or not as you like, I will not force you; but the fellow Ward, you shall never see again: remember, let his name never be mentioned again."

Roused to indignation, the Major spoke in a voice his daughter had never before heard from him, but at its tone her own spirit rose, and with a proud toss of her head she answered scornfully—

"Very well, father; but I tell you, you will be sorry for this; you will be sorry when it is too late." And then they parted— the parents and child—with bitter, angry feelings in each of their hearts.

CHAPTER LIII.

*I leave myself, my friends, and all for Love,
Thou, thou hast metamorphos'd me.*
SHAKSPEARE.

WITH a dreary moaning sound the wind swept round the strong gables of Leagh Bawn, rattling down the chimneys and whistling through the chinks of the latticed windows. In a small turret chamber, Isma O'Neil sat, dreamily watching the gaunt branches of the large trees, as they swayed backwards and forwards in the white moonlight. It was a cold, comfortless scene; but the girl's heart was warm with love and hope, and it seemed to her as if the prospect she looked on was but a shadow of her past life. Bright sunlit days she pictured to herself for the future which lay before her unspread, and the dismal sounds and sights of the present could not cloud over the pleasant dreams. Conn had gone, but not without promises and arrangements for a speedy return; her aunt, abstracted and pre-occupied with other thoughts, had yielded to the young man's arguments, and given a tacit consent to their marriage, when and how it pleased them. It was quite enough, she thought, to have the weight of her daughter's affairs on her hands, without involving herself in a contest with her niece, for whom she could have but little attachment.

"Ah! but it's a wild night and no mistake, Mistress Isma acushla!" said Winny, joining the young lady in her watch at the window. "Listen to the howling of the blast, and the creaking of them bare branches, mistress. Ohone, ohone, it's a cruel night for folks to be abroad."

"It is a wild night, and I hope there are not many without a roof over their heads, Winny. It is a cold winter's night in earnest."

"There's many a one out to-night that cannot just help themselves, mistress; but it's not the likes o' them I was a-thinking of."

"What do you mean, Winny? I should think few people would care to venture out a night like this without sufficient reason."

"There's no lack of reason, I take it, mistress, but the creatures have hit on a sorry night to make the venture, God help them. Things have come to a pretty pass when they cannot bide for a quiet night, let alone to do the thing decent."

"I don't understand whom you are talking about, Winny. Who is out? And what is the matter?"

"Of course you don't; how could you, acushla. It's only myself knows a haporth about it; not that the whole world wont know soon enough, and then, God help them! is all I say."

"Help who, Winny? What do you mean?"

"They're well away now, the creatures! and it can't hurt them to let on to you, honey. The deed's done now, and more power to them, I say, for it's pluck like that a body likes to see sometimes."

"Winny! I'm sure something is wrong. My cousin! Where is she? Tell me, what is all this about?"

"It's easy enough to tell the tale, bless your innocent heart, mistress; but it will be no so light a job to undo the work that's going on to-night. Before the morning's light comes they'll have gone out of my lady's ken at any rate, and no mistake."

"Grace! Miss Colthurst! Gone? What is it, Winny?"

"Gone! and bedad and it's herself that's gone right away, and small blame to her or to him either, for the matter of that."

"Oh, Winny! why did you not tell me this before? What shall we do? How shall we get her back?"

"Back, indeed: there'll be no coming back for her. And why should there? She's with him that's the light of her eyes. And what matters the cold and the wind to the likes o' them?"

"How did it all happen? Tell me quickly, Winny. Something must be done."

"There'll not be much done now, I'm

thinking, and of course it all happened just natural-like, as how else should it? He comes and gives her the sign, and she's not the one to need a second bidding when the fancy takes her. 'Winny,' says she, 'give me my cloak,' and away she sped without a thought to do else, and I said, 'God speed the pair of ye,' as I watched them tearing away, and thought of my lady's wrath, could she see them as I did."

"Oh, Winny, what will she say?"

"Never you mind what she says. She had no right to make misery between them poor young creatures. Not but what the Captain's a bit wild, as I know well. But sure she liked him, and what else could they do?"

"Winny, I must tell them—my uncle and aunt; perhaps there may still be time to follow them."

"Ah! you may follow them fast and hard now, mistress, but ye'll not come up to them this blessed night, the Lord knows. They may as well save themselves the trouble, and bide aisy in their beds."

True enough it was ; and many miles from Leagh, away to the northward, they passed on. Winny was right; the step was taken, and there was no coming back. On and on they went, heedless of the cold, searching blast, tracking their way by the fitful light of the moon which before long disappeared and left them in the darkness; and still on they went, further and further from Leagh.

Excited and over-wrought, Grace scarcely thought of what she had done. Irritated beyond control by opposition, she had acted on the spur of the moment; and the consequences, be they what they might, never entered into her imagination. She was with him, that was all; and it was enough. Never again would the words of persuasion or command come between them; never again would they tell her to forget him: they were together for ever now; for good or for evil, who could tell?

Wild and reckless as Lindesay Ward was, there had been some calculation and foresight on his part in this affair, and he thought now, as they rode on almost in silence, that at last he had been successful. He had gained his point: Grace was his, and he had conquered—conquered her proud, haughty spirit, outwitted the calculations of her friends; and the troubles which had been thickening round him since the close of the war would vanish under this new stroke of luck. He had calculated the influence Grace's father would have to extricate him from his difficulties. By uniting himself with his daughter he saw a safe and easy way of clearing himself, and their union once safely accomplished, he counted on the Major's affection for his only daughter to overcome all previous objections, and to prompt him to set matters as straight and smooth for her as might be in his power.

"Aunt, what is to be done?" said Isma, as Mrs. Colthurst, her cold face colder and harder now than ever, came back from a consultation with her husband.

"Your uncle says nothing—nothing is to be done, and I say the same. Henceforth

Grace is lost to us. We must forget her."

"Forget her! Oh, aunt, you do not mean it!"

"Yes, I say I forget her;" but as she repeated the words, the sense of what she had said came home to her mind. Forget her child—Grace? No, it was impossible; she knew it was, and all the bitter reality of the misfortune broke down the cold, hardening heart.

"Oh, Grace, Grace," she said, "how could you do it?"

"Aunt, forgive her; she could not help it. I am sure she scarcely knew what she did."

"Isma, you do not know her self-will, her determination at all times to please herself, regardless of others."

"Then you cannot wonder at this, aunt."

"I do wonder—wonder how she has blinded herself completely against her own good in this. She knew how I had her interest at heart. She pretended to agree with me altogether till lately. I cannot understand it. I depended on her, trusted in her completely, and now——"

"It is hard, very hard for you, aunt; but she could not help it, she was infatuated."

"Isma, I do not understand such excuses for such an act," said Mrs. Colthurst, relapsing into all the usual hard severity of her nature; "and, what is more, I will not listen to them. Grace has forfeited all right to consideration from her father and me; for the future, I do not desire to hear her named in my presence."

CHAPTER LIV.

"Some pow'r invisible supports his soul,
And bears it up in all its wonted greatness."
ADDISON.

DECEMBER had come; many of the Irish troops who had declared for France had already sailed, and Cork was full of those who only waited their turn to embark. Crowds thronged the shore; the transport ships had come back from their first voyage, and were again filling fast with boatloads of emigrants eager to enter upon the new life. Slowly pacing up and down the wharves, watching the busy scene, we may recognise some of our friends—two happy, bright faces contrasting strangely with some of the weary, harassed countenances around them; and contrasting, too, with their companion, a grave, quiet figure, silent and abstracted amid their light-hearted chatter. Life was but just opening for them—these two—Conn and Isma. Only a few days had elapsed since their fate had been linked together for better for worse till death them should part, and, proud and happy in each other's love, the future appeared all brightness and hope to them.

"How the sun sparkles and dances on the water; see, Conn, is it not lovely?" said Isma, looking out towards the sea.

"Yes; it almost tempts one to wish they were going the voyage themselves. Would you like it, Isma?"

"The sea will not always be so bright, I fear, Conn; and I am quite content to stay on dry land for my part. But you would be going now, only for me."

"Yes, only for you Edward would not be going alone to seek his fortunes across the sea. What a spoil-sport you are, after all. Edward there thinks so, I am sure."

"Hush!" she said, softly; "it is heartless of us to be so merry when he is just going to leave us."

Colonel Scott had looked up at the sound

of his own name, and heard Isma's whispered remonstrance.

"Never mind," he said; "you two must not be saddened for me. It is I who am the spoil-sport, I fear; but this is the last day. After to-morrow you will not have my sober company to oppress you."

"To-morrow!" they both echoed.

"Yes; to-morrow our transport goes. See, there are my fellow-passengers embarking already."

"Why did you not tell us before," said Conn, almost reproachfully.

"Why should I have troubled you with the news; it was unnecessary. Besides, I scarcely knew myself much sooner."

Silently the three stood, apparently watching the boatloads pushing off from the shore, but in reality so occupied with their own thoughts that the present scene was but dimly present to each. Conn, thinking only of the separation to-morrow, dwelt with regret on the daily life without Edward, the absence of his ever-ready help and counsel, and the tender love, almost of a father, which had ever been his; while Isma recalled to mind the Colonel Scott she had first known, quiet and undemonstrative always, but without that dark shadow in his eyes, and those lines of trouble on his brow which told of a sorrow past—a sorrow which he and she alone knew of. Yes, he was changed; she could see it in his face and hear it in his voice, and it had been her doing; she had, unwittingly though it was, brought this change upon him. Suddenly looking up, their eyes met, and he saw the tender pity which filled her heart.

"Don't," he said, almost impetuously; "you must not sorrow so for me. I am going of my own free will to seek my fortune, as Conn says, and who knows what good luck may turn up? Your quiet life at home would be irksome to me."

"A quiet life irksome to you, brother. Why, what a change!" said Conn, surprised at his brother's tone.

"Yes, you and I have changed places, Conn. You must be the steady, respectable member of the family, now, with this little woman to guide you," he said playfully, determined to put away the sad thoughts which still haunted Isma's eyes. " You will have a great deal on hand now, Isma, more than you reckon, with this scapegrace brother of mine."

" Yes, indeed," said Conn, "and she will not have you either to help her. What will you do, Isma?"

" I know what you must do, Isma," said the elder brother; " you must go to Cousin Deborah for assistance. Conn never could resist one of her wholesome lectures. Now confess, Conn, Cousin Deborah was always too much for you in the old days?"

"That she was, but I expect she will have nothing to say to me now that I have got a little heretic wife. What do you say, Isma?"

" Yes, I am afraid it will be a shock to her," said Isma, with a sad tone still in her voice.

"Never fear, it will be all right," said Edward; "she will see as I do that you have got some one to tame you now, Conn, and reduce you to be a fitting representative of the family honour."

"What will become of all these poor people?" said Isma, her eyes wandering to the crowds of wretched women and children who pressed forward towards the boats.

"God knows!" said the Colonel. "It is a miserable sight. Do what he will, Sarsfield could never get passage room for so many."

"He has promised to do so, has he not?" she asked.

"Yes, the men refused to come if something of the sort was not done, and I fear it will be a terrible scene in the end."

And a terrible scene it was in truth. To find room for the numbers who flocked to the shore was an impossibility, frantic as they were with thoughts of desolate homes, fathers, brothers, sons gone, the land untilled, the country forsaken; they had no thought but to follow, or die widowed and orphaned in their native land.

CHAPTER LV.

"But farewell, King, sith thus thou wilt appear;
Freedom lives hence, and banishment is here."
SHAKSPEARE.

To-morrow had come, and a party stood on the deck of one of the vessels bound for France. Last words were being spoken, and last looks were passing between friends who were to part perhaps for ever. Conn and Isma were there to see the last of Edward, and the time had now come when they must return alone to the shore. The Earl of Lucan and his party formed part of the group, and good wishes had been expressed again and again with hope and even enthusiasm on all sides.

"Now, Conn, it is time," said Edward, quiet and self-controlled to the last.

"Isma, let me help you down; and now good-bye. Forget me, child," he said in a voice audible only to her. " It is best as it is—I feel it is—you could not help it; only make Conn happy now, and I am satisfied."

" You are good and kind to the last," she said, "and, oh! you must be happy in the end. Promise me you will—promise me you will not let the past spoil all your future."

" It is in God's hands," he said earnestly, " and I am content."

The last good-byes were said, and the boat pushed from the ship's side.

" Poor Edward!" said Conn, as they rowed towards the shore: " what will our world be without him?"

" And he is so lonely, going away by himself to a foreign land," said Isma, with tears in her eyes.

" Yes, why does he not marry? See, Isma, he has turned to speak to that girl, Mary Sarsfield. She is a handsome girl too, why on earth could they not make a match?"

" If they only would," said Isma, earnestly.

" I should indeed be glad; she is true, I

am sure. Your brother has always spoken well of her, has he not?"

"Yes, in a matter-of-fact sort of way, he has often; but I doubt if Edward could ever make up his mind to such a thing, though it would be the best thing he could do, decidedly, if he only took the notion into his head."

"It would, indeed; I wonder would Miss Sarsfield suit him?" she said doubtfully.

"That's the question, and would he suit her, is another, but there's no knowing what propinquity might do; they'll be thrown together pretty much now, and I don't see well how he could help admiring a girl like that."

They had reached the shore now, and the last boatload of emigrants was about to start. The ships were full almost to overflowing, and still the crowds on the beach seemed scarcely lessened. Slowly the heavily-laden boat was pushed out to sea, and a cry of bitter sorrow burst forth from the crowd: the last chance was over now, the last effort had been made in vain, and hope died in the lonely, saddened hearts left behind. The son's strong young arm had gone forth from the aged father and the widowed mother; the husband was taken from his helpless wife; the little children would never know a father's care again, nor the desolate girl a brother's love in all the long dreary days of hardship and struggle which were before them in their native land—a lonely and devastated land now it was.

Heart-piercing were the sounds which filled the air: the hardest and coldest among the spectators could not refrain from sympathizing. Isma, her eyes dim with tears, clung close to Conn. "Look, look," she said; "oh, Conn, save that wretched girl."

But it was too late. With wild streaming hair, a young girl had rushed forward from the crowd, with a half-mad cry of sorrow. "Stay, stay, he must not go without me; I am coming, coming! Oh, it is me, Bill; take me—take me with you. I will never trouble you again—never, never; only take me with you; I cannot live without you."

A tall, dark man, standing in the stern of the boat, started at the sound of her voice, and leaning over the side, he said with a gruff, half-choking voice—

"Go back, Mary, it's no use now, I told you so many a time afore. Go back, girl, to your mother; ye'll never see poor Bill Hogan again."

"You promised, Bill, you promised. I must go! I must see you, you know I have followed you till now, all these long weary days. I will not—I cannot go back!"

"Fool!" said the man, hoarsely, as he tried to disengage her hand from the rope to which she clung. "Let go, I say, there's no help for it."

"I cannot, I cannot! Nothing will make me leave you, Bill. Bill, think on your promise; take me with you now." With a death-like clasp she held on, and at the moment Isma had caught sight of her, a sudden blow from some one in the boat, as it was pushed off from the shore, shook her grasp and she fell moaning into the angry surf. Quickly the waves closed over her, and the boat went on, a few vigorous strokes sweeping it out of reach. The dark, rough man cowered down, hiding his face for a moment from the dreadful sight, and then, with one long look at the shore, he turned his face resolutely to the waiting vessel and the far-stretching sea before him.

It was Galloping Hogan, the wild Rapparee: henceforth a new life was his, and, let us hope, a steadier purpose influenced his future.

A new era, it would seem, had dawned at this time for all our friends. Far away in the North, Grace Colthurst, now Grace Ward, was beginning her married life. The excitement of the last few weeks had died away, and she had had time to consider the importance of the hasty step she had taken. She had time—yes, plenty of time, to look round the isolated, lonely house which was now to be her home, to wander restlessly through the half empty rooms, and gaze out with wistful eyes on the long range of barren, rugged hills which would henceforth be the limit of her prospect. There was time enough, too, to think over the months past, and scarcely could she believe herself to be the same light-hearted girl who had often so recklessly bemoaned the slowly passing days, and beguiled their tedium by careless trifling with another's steadfast heart. This was all over now; he had suffered and passed away, and she had lived to suffer too, and learn that love was a reality, not the passing fancy of an idle hour. And where were all her visions of enjoyment in the good things of this life—the ease and the luxury which she had so often vowed must be her lot. Was it true that she had bartered them for love— a love which she had mocked and trifled with in others. The sacrifice had seemed small when she had braved darkness and storm, and gone out to meet him whom it seemed she could not choose but love. Standing by his side in the little country church in the early morning light there was no regret, no shrinking as she laid her hand in his, and heard his clear voice vowing love and fealty to her, his chosen, his wife. Nor would she have it otherwise now; he was all to her that he promised; fully he satisfied her heart's desire; but for all that, there was an awakening from the fever of excitement which had had possession of her imagination the last few weeks. Tender thoughts of the home she had left, the father and the mother she had slighted, filled her mind, and at times the remembrance of her cousin's words of advice, " Only be patient and wait," rang in her ears. Perhaps if she had waited, her father would have seen reason, and won over her mother, and the desired end would have been accomplished without this anger, this bitter, dark cloud of self-reproach which must hang over her for ever. Would they ever forgive her—ever let her see them again? were the thoughts which racked her heart, and brought that restless, hopeless look over her beautiful features, usually so placid and sweet in their expression, as she sat in her new home, watching the hot embers of the wood-fire crackle and crumble away. She was alone, as was often the case now, Captain Ward's outdoor pursuits occupying his attention. The evening was closing in, and she listened anxiously for his return; but the hours slipped on, and still she was alone. He had never been so late before, and she anxiously paced backwards and forwards through the dimly-lit entrance hall, peering from time to time out into the dark night to catch the first glimpse of his figure wending homewards over the hill. Sick and tired with watching, she turned once more towards the sitting-room, and, piling up fresh logs on the fire, she cowered down by its side to enjoy the warm glow which was the only cheerful thing remaining in the lonely house. Half dozing, she sat on till the voice of the old man who, with his wife, acted as servants in the house, roused her to spring up. "What is it, Larry? The Captain—where is he? You startled me."

"There's more to startle you than my

ould voice, mistress," he said, with the easy familiarity of an old follower.

"What is the matter? Has your master not come home yet—quick, tell me, Larry."

"Not home yet! and it'll be longer so, I am thinking, by the same token. Look ye here, mistress, my words has come true, as I always told thim they would. A body canna put his fingers in the fire without a singeing thim, and many a time I've told the Captain, God bless him, that he was meddling with what he shouldn't. But the young blood's uncommon hard to rule: he let it take its own gate, and now he's got himself into a pretty kettle o' fish, and no mistake."

"Oh, tell me what is wrong quickly, Larry. Where is he? Is he in danger?"

"The Lord knows, young lady! It's not for the likes o' me to say where there's danger in the wind or where there's nought, but this I know, if the young master had hearkened to many a bit of a word I ventured on, he'd not be in this quandary this blessed hour."

"What is it? I don't know, I don't understand?" said Grace, half wild with forebodings of what might have happened.

"Understand, how could you, you poor young creature? But look here, he bid me give you this, and break the news gentle-like to you, so you see I was afeared to be too smart in letting on to you." Eagerly Grace took from the old man's hand a scrap of paper, and bending down towards the fire-light, read its contents, which were as follow:—

"Dearest Grace.—The rogues have come down on me. Larry will explain all. There is nothing for it but to submit, and I will outwit them in the end. Write to your father to help me, it is all you can do. Take care of yourself: we shall soon be together again. Ever yours,

"L. W."

As mystified as ever, Grace turned to the old man for the promised explanation, which in his own roundabout way he at last made her understand. The indictments against

Captain Ward's lawless conduct during the war had been brought to bear on him: he had been followed to his retreat, and carried off by the officers of justice to stand his trial. Poor Grace was bewildered. She scarcely knew what to do or think about the matter, and then, remembering the injunction to communicate with her father, she sat down to a task which could not but be a mortifying and painful one to her proud nature, softening now, however, in the dreary sense of desolation which crept over her. She had written before, when she had first found herself in her husband's house, a half-defiant announcement of her marriage, but she had received no answer. Different, far different were her earnest entreaties now for reconciliation and help from the father whom she had so lately left in passion and bitterness.

Lonely days passed for her, days in which no tidings reached her from the outer world. All was still and silent. It seemed as if she were forsaken by all whom she had ever known or loved. In the long hours she lived again and again her past life, and thought with sorrow of the home she had left so lightly, and of the love in that home which she had valued so carelessly. Still her love for her husband was not weakened even by the disgrace which had fallen upon him; to help him and to rescue him she would do anything But what could she do? Nothing. She must wait and watch for the light which might still come.

CHAPTER LVI.

> " Behold, we know not anything;
> I can but trust that good shall fall
> At last—far off—at last, to all,
> And every winter turn to spring."—TENNYSON.

AND the light did come at last. The lonely house was once more roused by another step, and a loud cheery voice rang again through the silent rooms.

Major Colthurst could not find it in his heart to resist the sorrowful words of Grace's pleading for help: the thought of the girl, lonely and miserable far away from all her friends, touched his heart, and perhaps his wife's heart too, for he met with but little resistance to his proposal to seek his daughter out at once, and see what steps could be taken to save her. So he came and found her out in her lonely home, and cheered and comforted her with news of her husband. The trial must go on; but measures could be taken to avert any serious issue, and as the Major said, "Never mind, my dear, it will do the fellow all the good in the world, this little taste of discipline: you'll find him twice as easy to live with afterwards, take my word for it. Cheer up, Grace, my girl. We'll pull him through somehow, and, after all, I know myself pretty well what temptations a young fellow like him may have. You were a fool, Grace, not to take Manus. This is a tumbledown sort of an old place, but we must see what we can do about stocking the bawn yonder, and it's not an ugly stretch of land into that glen. You're pale, girl; look up and give your old father a kiss, and he'll set it all straight for you."

"Oh, father, you're too good. I don't deserve this forbearance."

" Very few of us do in our turn, Grace. You have not been much more foolish than the rest of us, only you and your mother there thought you could be twice as wise as the world in general. But it's not so easy to get away from our humanity, Grace, that's all need be said."

And so with this prospect of a happy future we must leave Grace. The past few weeks had taught her many a lesson which a lifetime of prosperity might not have done. In the days to come, the love which seemed to have brought so much trouble upon her was the guiding star of her life, influencing and steadying not only her own wayward will, but ruling with magic power the man whom she loved. His wild oats were sown too, and their consequences, more serious far than he had ever dreamt of, and needing all the Major's influence to modify, had the effect of sobering his reckless spirit: in the end we may hope that he settled down as a proper and respectable member of society.

But a few words remain to be said about the future of our other friends. Conn and Isma loved and lived together to the end of the chapter, cheering the last days of Cousin Deborah's lonely life ; and, it is to be hoped, profiting not a little by the good woman's ever-ready word of counsel. Edward Scott we cannot do better than leave as we last saw him, sailing away to a foreign country and still gazing at the shore he has left with wistful, saddened eyes. He is fast losing sight of those most dear to him on earth, and the home where his happiest days have been spent. Before him there is a new life—a changed scene—and we may trust that new hopes dawned for him, and that fresh ties were formed, which, though not as bright, were perhaps as true as those he had left in his own native land. Another sailing in the same ship was leaving much behind too. All her young enthusiasm for her country, all her glowing day-dreams, had been disappointed: her faith in what she had held to be most true had been broken down, soiled, and trampled in the dust. But she was young; and we can leave her too, trusting that she still found much to believe and hope in; and brightened perhaps the life of the man who stood with sorrowful eyes and heavy heart at her side, as together they watched the last glimpse of the land they both loved disappear in the distance.

And as for the future of Winny and Drummer Will, we need scarcely draw much on our imagination. Suffice it to say that they found riding double by no means an uncomfortable means of locomotion in the years to come; and that they set a ready example of mutual good-will to other hostile parties in Ireland by a speedy union, in which beauty and wit, as Will remarked, were successfully paired.

Last, not least, our old friend Sir Teague and his trusty companion Louis effected a reconciliation after the bold assertion of free-will on Louis' part on the memorable day of decision, when a difference of opinion divided them for a time. A mutual accommodation, however, was agreed upon; and, retiring into private life, they managed to tolerate each other's peculiarities of temperament till death laid them both to rest, faithful friends and companions to the last.

THE END.

TINSLEYS' MAGAZINE,

An Illustrated Monthly,
Price One Shilling.

Now publishing,

A PAIR OF BLUE EYES. By the Author of "Under the Greenwood Tree," "Desperate Remedies," &c.
LONDON'S HEART. By the Author of "Grif," "Joshua Marvel," and "Blade-o'-Grass."
HOME, SWEET HOME. A new Serial Story.
MUSICAL RECOLLECTIONS OF THE LAST HALF CENTURY.
MODERN VERSIONS OF THE CLASSICS.

The first Ten Volumes of "Tinsleys' Magazine" are now ready,
Containing:

UNDER THE RED DRAGON. A complete Novel. By JAMES GRANT, author of "The Romance of War," "Only an Ensign," &c.
THE MONARCH OF MINCING LANE. A complete Novel. By the Author of "The Daughter of Heth," &c.
GEORGE CANTERBURY'S WILL. A complete Novel. By Mrs. HENRY WOOD, author of "East Lynne," &c.
THE ROCK AHEAD. A complete Novel. By EDMUND YATES, author of "Black Sheep," &c.
BREAKING A BUTTERFLY. A complete Novel. By the Author of "Guy Livingstone," &c.
AUSTIN FRIARS. A complete Novel. By Mrs. J. H. RIDDELL, author of "George Geith," &c.
JOSHUA MARVEL. A complete Novel. By B. L. FARJEON, author of "Grif," &c.
LADY JUDITH. A complete Novel. By JUSTIN MCCARTHY, author of "My Enemy's Daughter," &c.
A HOUSE OF CARDS. A complete Novel. By Mrs. CASHEL HOEY, author of "Falsely True," &c.
DOCTOR BRADY. A complete Novel. By W. H. RUSSELL, LL.D., of the *Times.*
THE HON. ALICE BRAND'S CORRESPONDENCE.
And numerous Essays and Articles by Popular Authors.

The above Volumes are elegantly bound in cloth gilt, price 8s. per volume. Cases for Binding may be had of the Publisher, price 1s. 6d. each.

TINSLEY BROTHERS, 18 CATHERINE STREET, STRAND.

TINSLEY BROTHERS' LIST OF NEW BOOKS.

A New and Important Book of Travels.

Unexplored Syria. By Capt. BURTON, F.R.G.S., and Mr. C. F. TYRWHITT DRAKE, F.R.G.S.. &c. With a New Map of Syria, Illustrations, Inscriptions, the 'Hamah Stones,' &c. 2 vols. 8vo, 32s.

"The work before us is no common book of travels. It is rather a series of elaborate, and at the same time luminous, descriptions of the various sites visited and explored by the authors, either together or singly, and of the discoveries made there by them.... The present joint production of Captain Burton and Mr. Tyrwhitt-Drake is therefore most opportune, on account of the material additions it makes to our acquaintance with a region which, notwithstanding the deep interest it excites, is still but imperfectly explored."—*Athenæum*.

"While these magnificent volumes, with their original plans and sketches by Mr. Drake, the unrivalled map of Northern Syria, and the luxurious print, are triumphs of typography, they are at the same time enduring monuments of the energy and enterprise of our countrymen."—*John Bull*.

"The book must be pronounced to be valuable for its information."—*Spectator*.

The Recollections and Reflections of J. R. PLANCHÉ
(*Somerset Herald*). A Professional Autobiography. 2 vols. 8vo, 25s.

"Besides illustrations of social and dramatic life, of literature, and of authors, Mr. Planché gives us record of travels, incidents of his *other* professional life as a herald, and reflections on most matters which have come under his notice. We have only now to leave Mr. Planché and his book to an appreciating public. There are few men who have amused and delighted the public as long as he has done; and perhaps there has never been a dramatic writer who has been so distinguished as he has been for uniting the utmost amount of wit and humour with refinement of expression and perfect purity of sentiment."—*Athenæum*.

"We have here two goodly octavo volumes full of amusing and often instructive gossip. To the portions of his book which will chiefly interest the general reader we have scarcely adverted at all. simply because we know not how to deal with them. So many and so good are the anecdotes he relates, that two or three could not be taken from the rest by any process more critical than the toss of a halfpenny."—*Saturday Review*.

Uniform with the above,

Musical Recollections of the Last Half-Century.
2 vols. 8vo.

The Life and Times of Algernon Sydney, Patriot,
1617—1683. By ALEXANDER CHARLES EWALD, F.S.A.. Senior Clerk of Her Majesty's Public Records, author of "The Crown and its Advisers," "Last Century of Universal History," &c. 2 vols. 8vo.

The Life and Times of Margaret of Anjou. By
Mrs. HOOKHAM. 2 vols. 8vo, 30s.

"Let Mrs Hookham's history be as largely circulated as possible, and earnestly read in every home."—*Bell's Weekly Messenger*.

"The collection of the materials has evidently been a laborious task; the composition is careful and conscientious throughout, and it contains a great deal that is valuable and highly interesting."—*Pall Mall Gazette*.

TINSLEY BROTHERS, 18 CATHERINE STREET, STRAND.

TINSLEY BROTHERS' LIST OF NEW BOOKS.

Baron Grimbosh: Doctor of Philosophy and sometime Governor of Barataria. A Record of his Experiences, written by himself in Exile, and Published by Authority. 1 vol. 8vo, 10s. 6d.

"Grimbosh, in Barataria, is surrounded by certain counsellors and others, whose identity is transparent through their pseudonyms. A couple of hours may be well spent in taking in the wit, the wisdom, the fun, and the folly, which flare up about them, from the overture to the fall of the curtain."—*Athenæum.*

The Court of Anna Carafa: an Historical Narrative. By Mrs. St. John. 1 vol. 8vo, 12s.

"Apart from the interest which centres around the fair Duchess of Medina, we obtain much curious and valuable information concerning the political intrigues of Spain and Italy during the first half of the seventeenth century. This is a deeply interesting and highly instructive volume."—*Court Journal.*

The Newspaper Press: its Origin, Progress, and Present Position. By James Grant, author of "Random Recollections," "The Great Metropolis," &c., and late Editor of the *Morning Advertiser.* 2 vols. 8vo, 30s.

"It was natural that such a man, to whom the press had been, as it were, the atmosphere he had breathed for half a lifetime, should think of recording what he personally knew, or had historically gathered, concerning that unique institution."—*Standard.*

Under the Sun. By George Augustus Sala, author of "My Diary in America," &c. 1 vol. 8vo, 15s.

"We can loiter pleasantly enough with him in the streets and lanes, on the wharfs and courtyards, and we find much to entertain us in his picture of the humours of Havana."—*Athenæum.*

Military Men I have Met. By E. Dyne Fenton, author of "Sorties from Gib." With Twenty Illustrations. 1 vol. 8vo, 7s. 6d.

"Captain Fenton, encouraged by the very favourable reception which, with hardly an exception, his first essay in military writing received, has wisely ventured on another volume, in which he sketches, with all the brevity, and not unfrequently with much of the wit, of Theophrastus, portraits of the military men he has met with in his military career ..... The illustrations by Sambourne are excellent and laughter-moving."—*Bell's Weekly Messenger.*

The Life and Adventures of Alexander Dumas. By Percy Fitzgerald, author of "The Lives of the Kembles," &c. 2 vols. 8vo.

Paris after Two Sieges. Notes of a Visit during the Armistice and immediately after the Suppression of the Commune. By William Woodall. 1 vol. [*Just ready.*

Judicial Dramas: Romances of French Criminal Law. By Henry Spicer. 1 vol. 8vo, 15s.

The Retention of India. By Alexander Halliday. 1 vol. 7s. 6d.

TINSLEY BROTHERS, 18 CATHERINE STREET, STRAND.

WORKS BY CAPTAIN BURTON, F.R.G.S. &c.

A New Book of Travels.

Zanzibar. By CAPTAIN R. F. BURTON, author of "A Mission to Geléle," "Explorations of the Highlands of the Brazil," "Abeokuta," "My Wanderings in West Africa," &c. 30s.

"We welcome with pleasure this new work from the prolific pen of the accomplished traveller in all four quarters of the globe. The information furnished is unquestionably very valuable and interesting."—*Athenæum*.

Explorations of the Highlands of the Brazil; with a full account of the Gold and Diamond Mines; also, Canoeing down Fifteen Hundred Miles of the great River, Sao Francisco, from Sabará to the Sea. In 2 vols. 8vo, with Map and Illustrations, 30s.

A Mission to Geléle. Being a Three Months' Residence at the Court of Dahomé. In which are described the Manners and Customs of the Country, including the Human Sacrifice, &c. 2 vols., with Illustrations, 25s.

Abeokuta; and an Exploration of the Cameroons Mountains. 2 vols, post 8vo, with Portrait of the Author, Map, and Illustrations. 25s.

Wit and Wisdom from West Africa; or a Book of Proverbial Philosophy, Idioms, Enigmas, and Laconisms. Compiled by RICHARD F. BURTON, author of "A Mission to Dahomé," "A Pilgrimage to El-Medinah and Meccah," &c. 12s. 6d.

My Wanderings in West Africa; from Liverpool to Fernando Po. 2 vols. cr. 8vo, 21s.

Letters from the Battle-fields of Paraguay. With Map and Illustrations, 18s.

The Nile Basin. With Map, &c. post 8vo, 7s. 6d.

WORKS BY GEORGE AUGUSTUS SALA.

My Diary in America in the Midst of War. In 2 vols. 8vo, 30s.

Notes and Sketches of the Paris Exhibition. 8vo, 15s.

From Waterloo to the Peninsula. 2 vols. 8vo, 24s.

Rome and Venice, with other Wanderings in Italy, in 1866-7. 8vo, 16s.

Accepted Addresses. 1 vol. cr. 8vo, 5s.

TINSLEY BROTHERS, 18 CATHERINE STREET, STRAND.

History of France under the Bourbons, 1589-1830.
By CHARLES DUKE YONGE, Regius Professor, Queen's College, Belfast. In 4 vols. 8vo. Vols. I. and II. contain the Reigns of Henry IV., Louis XIII. and XIV.; Vols. III. and IV. contain the Reigns of Louis XV. and XVI. 3*l.*

The Regency of Anne of Austria, Queen of France,
Mother of Louis XIV. From Published and Unpublished Sources. With Portrait. By Miss FREER. 2 vols. 8vo, 30*s.*

The Married Life of Anne of Austria, Queen of
France, Mother of Louis XIV.; and the History of Don Sebastian, King of Portugal. Historical Studies. From numerous Unpublished Sources. By MARTHA WALKER FREER. 2 vols. 8vo, 30*s.*

The History of Monaco. By H. PEMBERTON. 12*s.*

The Great Country: Impressions of America. By
GEORGE ROSE, M.A. (ARTHUR SKETCHLEY). 8vo, 15*s.*

Biographies and Portraits of some Celebrated
People. By ALPHONSE DE LAMARTINE. 2 vols. 25*s.*

Memoirs of the Life and Reign of George III.
With Original Letters of the King and Other Unpublished MSS. By J. HENEAGE JESSE, author of "The Court of England under the Stuarts," &c. 3 vols. 8vo. £2 2*s.* Second Edition.

The Public Life of Lord Macaulay. By FREDERICK
ARNOLD, B.A. of Christ Church, Oxford. Post 8vo, 7*s.* 6*d.*

Memoirs of Sir George Sinclair, Bart., of Ulbster.
By JAMES GRANT, author of "The Great Metropolis," "The Religious Tendencies of the Times," &c. 8vo. With Portrait. 16*s.*

Memories of My Time; being Personal Reminiscences of Eminent Men. By GEORGE HODDER. 8vo. 16*s.*

Lives of the Kembles. By PERCY FITZGERALD,
author of the "Life of David Garrick," &c. 2 vols. 8vo. 30*s.*

The Life of David Garrick. From Original Family
Papers, and numerous Published and Unpublished Sources. By PERCY FITZGERALD, M.A. 2 vols. 8vo, with Portraits. 30*s.*

The Life of Edmund Kean. From various Published and Original Sources. By F. W. HAWKINS. In 2 vols. 8vo, 30*s.*

Our Living Poets: an Essay in Criticism. By
H. BUXTON FORMAN. 1 vol., 12*s.*

Johnny Robinson: The Story of the Childhood and
Schooldays of an "Intelligent Artisan." By the Author of "Some Habits and Customs of the Working Classes." 2 vols. 21*s.*

TINSLEY BROTHERS, 18 CATHERINE STREET, STRAND.

Letters on International Relations before and during
the War of 1870. By the *Times* Correspondent at Berlin. Reprinted,
by permission, from the *Times*, with considerable Additions. 2 vols.
8vo. 30s.

The Story of the Diamond Necklace. By HENRY
VIZETELLY. Illustrated with an exact representation of the Diamond Necklace, and a Portrait of the Countess de la Motte, engraved
on steel. 2 vols. post 8vo, 25s. Second Edition.

English Photographs. By an American. 8vo, 12s.

Travels in Central Africa, and Exploration of the
Western Nile Tributaries. By Mr. and Mrs. PETHERICK. With
Maps, Portraits, and numerous Illustrations. 2 vols. 8vo, 25s.

From Calcutta to the Snowy Range. By an OLD
INDIAN. With numerous coloured Illustrations. 14s.

Stray Leaves of Science and Folk-lore. By J. SCOFFERN, M.B. Lond. 8vo. 12s.

Three Hundred Years of a Norman House. With
Genealogical Miscellanies. By JAMES HANNAY, author of "A
Course of English Literature," "Satire and Satirists," &c. 12s.

The Religious Life of London. By J. EWING RITCHIE,
author of the "Night Side of London," &c. 8vo. 12s.

Religious Thought in Germany. By the TIMES
CORRESPONDENT at Berlin. Reprinted from the *Times*. 8vo. 12s.

Mornings of the Recess in 1861-4. Being a Series
of Literary and Biographical Papers, reprinted from the *Times*, by
permission, and revised by the Author. 2 vols. 21s.

The Schleswig-Holstein War. By EDWARD DICEY,
author of "Rome in 1860." 2 vols. 16s.

The Battle-fields of 1866. By EDWARD DICEY,
author of "Rome in 1860," &c. 12s.

From Sedan to Saarbrück, viâ Verdun, Gravelotte,
and Metz. By an Officer of the Royal Artillery. In one vol. 7s. 6d.

British Senators; or Political Sketches, Past and
Present. By J. EWING RITCHIE. Post 8vo, 10s. 6d.

Prohibitory Legislation in the United States. By
JUSTIN MCCARTHY. 1 vol., 2s. 6d.

The Idol in Horeb. Evidence that the Golden
Image at Mount Sinai was a Cone and not a Calf. With Three Appendices. By CHARLES T. BEKE, Ph.D. 1 vol., 5s.

TINSLEY BROTHERS, 18 CATHERINE STREET, STRAND.

Ten Years in Sarawak. By CHARLES BROOKE, the "Tuanmudah" of Sarawak. With an Introduction by H. H. the Rajah Sir JAMES BROOKE; and numerous Illustrations. 2 vols. 25s.

Peasant Life in Sweden. By L. LLOYD, author of "The Game Birds of Sweden," "Scandinavian Adventures," &c. 8vo. With Illustrations. 18s.

Hog Hunting in the East, and other Sports. By Captain J. NEWALL, author of "The Eastern Hunters." With numerous Illustrations. 8vo, 21s.

The Eastern Hunters. By Captain JAMES NEWALL. 8vo, with numerous Illustrations. 16s.

Fish Hatching; and the Artificial Culture of Fish. By FRANK BUCKLAND. With 5 Illustrations. 5s.

Incidents in my Life. By D. D. Home. In 1 vol. crown 8vo, 10s. 6d. Second Series.

Con Amore; or, Critical Chapters. By JUSTIN MCCARTHY, author of "The Waterdale Neighbours." Post 8vo. 12s.

The Cruise of the Humming Bird, being a Yacht Cruise around the West Coast of Ireland. By MARK HUTTON. In 1 vol. 14s.

Murmurings in the May and Summer of Manhood: O'Ruark's Bride, or the Blood-spark in the Emerald; and Man's Mission a Pilgrimage to Glory's Goal. By EDMUND FALCONER. 1 vol., 5s.

Poems. By EDMUND FALCONER. 1 vol., 5s.

Dante's Divina Commedia. Translated into English in the Metre and Triple Rhyme of the Original. By Mrs. RAMSAY. 3 vols. 18s.

The Gaming Table, its Votaries and Victims, in all Countries and Times, especially in England and France. By ANDREW STEINMETZ, Barrister-at-Law. 2 vols. 8vo. 31s.

Principles of Comedy and Dramatic Effect. By PERCY FITZGERALD, author of "The Life of Garrick," &c. 8vo. 12s.

A Winter Tour in Spain. By the Author of "Altogether Wrong." 8vo, illustrated, 15s.

Life Beneath the Waves; and a Description of the Brighton Aquarium, with numerous Illustrations. 1 vol., 2s. 6d.

The Rose of Jericho; from the French; called by the German "Weinachts-Rose," or "Christmas Rose. Edited by the Hon. Mrs. NORTON, Author of "Old Sir Douglas," &c. 2s. 6d.

The Bells: a Romantic Story. Adapted from the French of MM. ERCKMANN-CHATRIAN. 1s.

TINSLEY BROTHERS, 18 CATHERINE STREET, STRAND.

TINSLEY BROTHERS'
SERIES OF SEVEN-AND-SIXPENNY WORKS.

HANDSOMELY BOUND IN BEVELLED BOARDS.

Poppies in the Corn; or Glad Hours in the Grave Years. By the Author of "The Harvest of a Quiet Eye," &c.

The Pilgrim and the Shrine; or Passages from the Life and Correspondence of Herbert Ainslie, B.A., Cantab.

Higher Law. A Romance in One Volume.

Moorland and Stream. By W. BARRY.

Maxims by a Man of the World. By the Author of "Lost Sir Massingberd."

The Adventures of a Bric-a-Brac Hunter. By Major BYNG HALL.

The Night Side of London. By J. EWING RITCHIE, author of "About London," &c. New and Enlarged Edition.

Some Habits and Customs of the Working Classes. By a JOURNEYMAN ENGINEER.

The Great Unwashed. By "THE JOURNEYMAN ENGINEER." Uniform with "Some Habits and Customs of the Working Classes."

Sunnyside Papers. By ANDREW HALLIDAY.

Essays in Defence of Women. Crown 8vo, handsomely bound in cloth, gilt, bevelled boards.

Places and People; being Studies from the Life. By J. C. PARKINSON.

A Course of English Literature. By JAMES HANNAY.
Suitable for Students and Schools.

Modern Characteristics: a Series of Essays from the "Saturday Review," revised by the Author.

The Law: What I have Seen, What I have Heard, and What I have Known. By CYRUS JAY.

The King of Topsy-Turvy: a Fairy Tale. By the Author of "The Enchanted Toasting-Fork." Profusely illustrated and handsomely bound. 5s.

The Enchanted Toasting-fork: a Fairy Tale. Profusely illustrated and handsomely bound. 5s.

TINSLEY BROTHERS, 18 CATHERINE STREET, STRAND.

TINSLEY BROTHERS'
CHEAP EDITIONS OF POPULAR NOVELS.

By Mrs. HENRY WOOD, author of "East Lynne," &c.

The Red Court Farm. 6s.
A Life's Secret. 6s.
George Canterbury's Will. 6s.
Anne Hereford. 6s.
Elster's Folly. 6s.
St. Martin's Eve. 6s.
Mildred Arkell. 6s.
Trevlyn Hold. 6s.

By the Author of "Guy Livingstone."

Sword and Gown. 5s.
Barren Honour. 6s.
Brakespeare. 6s.
Anteros. 6s.
Maurice Dering. 6s.
Guy Livingstone. 5s.
Sans Merci. 6s.
Border and Bastille. 6s.

Also, now ready, uniform with the above,

Old Margaret. By HENRY KINGSLEY, author of "Geoffry Hamlyn," "Hetty," &c.

The Harveys. By HENRY KINGSLEY, author of "Mademoiselle Mathilde," "Old Margaret," &c. 6s.

A Life's Assize. By Mrs. J. H. RIDDELL, author of "Too Much Alone," "City and Suburb," "George Geith," &c. 6s.

A Righted Wrong. By EDMUND YATES. 6s.

Stretton. By HENRY KINGSLEY, author of "Geoffry Hamlyn," &c. 6s.

The Rock Ahead. By EDMUND YATES. 6s.

The Adventures of Dr. Brady. By W. H. RUSSELL, LL.D. 6s.

Black Sheep. By EDMUND YATES, author of "The Rock Ahead," &c. 6s.

Kissing the Rod. By EDMUND YATES. 6s.

Not Wisely, but Too Well. By the Author of "Cometh up as a Flower." 6s.

Miss Forrester. By the Author of "Archie Lovell," &c. 6s.

Recommended to Mercy. By the Author of "Sink or Swim?" 6s.

Lizzie Lorton of Greyrigg. By Mrs. LYNN LINTON, author of "Sowing the Wind," &c. 6s.

The Seven Sons of Mammon. By G. A. SALA, author of "After Breakfast," &c. 6s.

Maxwell Drewitt. By Mrs. J. H. RIDDELL, author of "Too Much Alone," "A Life's Assize," &c. 6s.

Faces for Fortunes. By AUGUSTUS MAYHEW. 6s.

TINSLEYS' TWO-SHILLING VOLUMES,

Uniformly bound in Illustrated Wrappers.

To be had at every Railway Stall and of every Bookseller in the Kingdom.

By the Author of "Guy Livingstone."

Sword and Gown.	Breaking a Butterfly.
Maurice Dering.	Anteros.
Barren Honour.	Sans Merci.
Brakespeare.	

By EDMUND YATES.

A Righted Wrong.	Broken to Harness.
Black Sheep.	The Rock Ahead.

Also, uniform with the above,

The Cambridge Freshman; or Memoirs of Mr. Golightly. By MARTIN LEGRAND. With numerous Illustrations by PHIZ.

Old Margaret. By HENRY KINGSLEY, author of "Geoffry Hamlyn," "Hetty," &c.

Joshua Marvel. By B. L. FARJEON, author of "Grif," "London's Heart," and "Blade-o'-Grass."

Papers Humorous and Pathetic; being Selections from the Works of GEORGE AUGUSTUS SALA.

Gaslight and Daylight. By GEORGE AUGUSTUS SALA, author of "After Breakfast," "Dutch Pictures," &c.

Grif. By the Author of "Joshua Marvel," &c.

A Perfect Treasure. By the Author of "Lost Sir Massingberd."

Netherton-on-Sea. Edited by the late Dean of Canterbury.

My Enemy's Daughter. By JUSTIN MCCARTHY.

Love Stories of the English Watering-Places.

The Adventures of Dr. Brady. By W. H. RUSSELL, LL.D. (*Times* Special Correspondent).

Not Wisely, but Too Well. By the Author of "Cometh up as a Flower."

Recommended to Mercy. By the Author of "Sink or Swim?"

The Waterdale Neighbours. By JUSTIN MCCARTHY.

The Pretty Widow. By CHARLES H. ROSS.

Miss Forrester. By the Author of 'Archie Lovell.'

The Dower-House. By ANNIE THOMAS.

The Savage-Club Papers (1867). With all the Original Illustrations. Also the Second Series, for 1868.

Every-day Papers. By ANDREW HALLIDAY.

☞ *The above may also be had, handsomely bound in cloth, 2s. 6d. per volume.*

TINSLEY BROTHERS' NEW NOVELS
AT EVERY LIBRARY.

Notice.—A New Novel by Harrison Ainsworth.

Boscobel: a Tale of the Year 1651. By WILLIAM HARRISON AINSWORTH, author of "Rookwood," "The Tower of London," &c. With Illustrations. 3 vols.

At His Gates. By Mrs. OLIPHANT, author of "Chronicles of Carlingford," &c.

The Vicar's Daughter: a New Story. By GEORGE MACDONALD, author of "Annals of a Quiet Neighbourhood," "The Seaboard Parish," &c.

A Waiting Race. By EDMUND YATES, author of "Broken to Harness," "Black Sheep," &c. 3 vols.

Valentin: a Story of Sedan. By HENRY KINGSLEY, author of "Ravenshoe," "Geoffry Hamlyn," &c. 2 vols.

Two Worlds of Fashion. By CALTHORPE STRANGE.

The Pace that Kills: a New Novel. 3 vols.

A Woman's Triumph. By Lady HARDY. 3 vols.

Erma's Engagements: a New Novel. By the Author of "Blanche Seymour," &c.

Dower and Curse. By JOHN LANE FORD, author of "Charles Stennie," &c.

Autobiography of a Cornish Rector. By the late JAMES HAMLEY TREGENNA. 2 vols.

The Scarborough Belle. By ALICE CHARLOTTE SAMPSON. 3 vols.

Puppets Dallying. By ARTHUR LILLIE, author of "Out of the Meshes," "King of Topsy Turvy," &c.

Under the Greenwood Tree. A Rural Painting of the Dutch School. By the Author of "Desperate Remedies," &c. 2 vols.

Coming Home to Roost. By GERALD GRANT. 3 vols.

Midnight Webs. By G. M. FENN, author of "The Sapphire Cross," &c. 1 vol. fancy cloth binding, 10s. 6d.

Sorties from "Gib." in quest of Sensation and Sentiment. By E. DYNE FENTON, late Captain 86th Regiment. 1 vol. post 8vo, 10s. 6d.

TINSLEY BROTHERS, 18 CATHERINE STREET, STRAND.

The Golden Lion of Granpere. By ANTHONY TROLLOPE, author of "Ralph the Heir," "Can You Forgive Her?" &c.

Under which King. By B. W. JOHNSTON, M.P. 1 vol.

Under the Red Dragon. By JAMES GRANT, author of "The Romance of War," "Only an Ensign," &c.

Hornby Mills; and other Stories. By HENRY KINGSLEY, author of "Ravenshoe," "Mademoiselle Mathilde," "Geoffry Hamlyn," &c. In 2 vols.

Grainger's Thorn. By THOS. WRIGHT (the "Journeyman Engineer"), author of "The Bane of a Life," "Some Habits and Customs of the Working Classes," &c. 3 vols.

Church and Wife: a Question of Celibacy. By ROBERT ST. JOHN CORBET, author of "The Canon's Daughters." 3 vols.

Not Easily Jealous: a New Novel. In 3 vols.

Rough but True. By ST. CLARE. In 1 vol.

Christopher Dudley. By MARY BRIDGMAN, author of 'Robert Lynne,' &c. In 3 vols.

Love and Treason. By W. FREELAND. 3 vols.

Tender Tyrants. By JOSEPH VEREY. 3 vols.

Loyal: a New Novel. By M. A. GODFREY. 3 vols.

Fatal Sacrifice: a New Novel.

Old Margaret. By HENRY KINGSLEY, author of "Ravenshoe," "Geoffry Hamlyn," &c. 2 vols.

Bide Time and Tide. By J. T. NEWALL, author of "The Gage of Honour," "The Eastern Hunters," &c. 3 vols.

The Scandinavian Ring. By JOHN POMEROY. 3 vols.

The Harveys. By HENRY KINGSLEY, author of "Old Margaret," "Hetty," "Geoffry Hamlyn," &c. 2 vols.

TINSLEY BROTHERS, 18 CATHERINE STREET, STRAND.

Henry Ancrum: a Tale of the last War in New Zealand. 2 vols.

She was Young, and He was Old. By the Author of "Lover and Husband." 3 vols.

A Ready-made Family: or the Life and Adventures of Julian Leep's Cherub. A Story. 3 vols.

Cecil's Tryst. By the Author of "Lost Sir Massingberd," &c. 3 vols.

Denison's Wife. By Mrs. ALEXANDER FRASER, author of "Not while She lives," "Faithless; or the Loves of the Period," &c. 2 vols.

Barbara Heathcote's Trial. By the Author of "Nellie's Memories," &c. 3 vols.

Wide of the Mark. By the Author of "Recommended to Mercy," "Taken upon Trust," &c. 3 vols.

Title and Estate. By F. LANCASTER. 3 vols.

Hollowhill Farm. By JOHN EDWARDSON. 3 vols.

The Sapphire Cross: a Tale of Two Generations. By G. M. FENN, author of "Bent, not Broken," &c. 3 vols.

Edith. By C. A. LEE. 2 vols.

Lady Judith. By JUSTIN McCARTHY, author of "My Enemy's Daughter," "The Waterdale Neighbours," &c. 3 vols.

Only an Ensign. By JAMES GRANT, author of "The Romance of War," "Lady Wedderburn's Wish," &c. 3 vols.

Old as the Hills. By DOUGLAS MOREY FORD. 3 vols.

Not Wooed, but Won. By the Author of "Lost Sir Massingberd," "Found Dead," &c. 3 vols.

My Heroine. 1 vol.

Sundered Lives. By WYBERT REEVE, author of the Comedies of "Won at Last," "Not so Bad after all," &c. 3 vols.

TINSLEY BROTHERS, 18 CATHERINE STREET, STRAND.

The Prussian Spy. By V. VALMONT. 2 vols.

The Nomads of the North: a Tale of Lapland. By J. LOVEL HADWEN. 1 vol.

Family Pride. By the Author of "Olive Varcoe," "Simple as a Dove," &c. 3 vols.

Fair Passions; or the Setting of the Pearls. By the Hon. Mrs. PIGOTT CARLETON. 3 vols.

Harry Disney: an Autobiography. Edited by ATHOLL DE WALDEN. 3 vols.

Desperate Remedies. 3 vols.

The Foster Sisters. By EDMOND BRENAN LOUGHNAN. 3 vols.

Only a Commoner. By HENRY MORFORD. 3 vols.

Madame la Marquise. By the Author of "Dacia Singleton," "What Money Can't Do," &c. 3 vols.

Clara Delamaine. By A. W. CUNNINGHAM. 3 vols.

Sentenced by Fate. By Miss EDGCOMBE. 3 vols.

Fairly Won. By Miss H. S. ENGSTRÖM. 3 vols.

Joshua Marvel. By B. L. FARJEON, author of "Grif." 3 vols.

Blanche Seymour. 3 vols.

By Birth a Lady. By G. M. FENN, author of "Mad," "Webs in the Way," &c. 3 vols.

A Life's Assize. By Mrs. J. H. RIDDELL, author of "George Geith," "City and Suburb," "Too much Alone," &c. 3 vols.

Gerald Hastings. By the Author of "No Appeal," &c. 3 vols.

Monarch of Mincing-Lane. By WILLIAM BLACK, author of "In Silk Attire," "Kilmeny," &c. 3 vols.

TINSLEY BROTHERS, 18 CATHERINE STREET, STRAND.

The Golden Bait. By H. HOLL, author of "The King's Mail," &c. In 3 vols.

Like Father, like Son. By the Author of "Lost Sir Massingberd," &c. 3 vols.

Beyond these Voices. By the EARL OF DESART, author of "Only a Woman's Love," &c. 3 vols.

The Queen's Sailors. A Nautical Novel. By EDWARD GREEY. 3 vols.

Bought with a Price. By the Author of "Golden Pippin," &c. 1 vol.

The Florentines: a Story of Home-life in Italy. By the COUNTESS MARIE MONTEMERLI, author of "Four Months in a Garibaldian Hospital," &c. 3 vols.

The Inquisitor. By WILLIAM GILBERT, author of "Doctor Austin's Guests," &c. 3 vols.

Falsely True. By Mrs. CASHEL HOEY, author of "A House of Cards," &c. In 3 vols.

After Baxtow's Death. By MORLEY FARROW, author of "No Easy Task," &c. 3 vols.

Hearts and Diamonds. By ELIZABETH P. RAMSAY, 3 vols.

The Bane of a Life. By THOMAS WRIGHT (the Journeyman Engineer), author of "Some Habits and Customs of the Working Classes," &c. 3 vols.

Robert Lynne. By MARY BRIDGMAN. 2 vols.

Baptised with a Curse. By EDITH S. DREWRY. 3 vols.

Brought to Book. By HENRY SPICER, Esq. 2 vols.

Fenacre Grange. By LANGFORD CECIL. 3 vols.

Schooled with Briars: a Story of To-day. 1 vol.

A Righted Wrong. By EDMUND YATES, author of "Black Sheep," &c. 3 vols.

TINSLEY BROTHERS, 18 CATHERINE STREET, STRAND.

Gwendoline's Harvest. By the Author of "Lost Sir Massingberd," "Found Dead," &c. 2 vols.

A Fool's Paradise. By THOMAS ARCHER, author of "Strange Work," &c. 3 vols.

George Canterbury's Will. By Mrs. HENRY WOOD, author of "East Lynne," &c. 3 vols.

Gold and Tinsel. By the Author of "Ups and Downs of an Old Maid's Life." 3 vols.

Sidney Bellew. A Sporting Story. By FRANCIS FRANCIS. 2 vols.

Ready-Money Mortiboy: a Matter of Fact Story. 3 vols.

Not while She Lives. By the Author of "Faithless; or the Loves of the Period." 2 vols.

A Double Secret and Golden Pippin. By JOHN POMEROY. 3 vols.

Heathfield Hall; or Prefatory Life. A Youthful Reminiscence. By HANS SCHREIBER, author of "Nicknames at the Playingfield College," &c. 10s. 6d.

Phœbe's Mother. By LOUISA ANN MEREDITH, author of "My Bush Friends in Tasmania." 2 vols.

Strong Hands and Steadfast Hearts. By the Countess von BOTHMER. 3 vols.

Saved by a Woman. By the Author of "No Appeal," &c. 3 vols.

Home from India. By JOHN POMEROY. 2 vols.

The Soul and Money: a New Novel. 1 vol. 7s. 6d.

Nellie's Memories: a Domestic Story. By ROSA NOUCHETTE CAREY. 3 vols.

Clarissa. By SAMUEL RICHARDSON. Edited by E. S. DALLAS, author of "The Gay Science," &c. 3 vols.

Tregarthen Hall. By JAMES GARLAND. 3 vols.

TINSLEY BROTHERS, 18 CATHERINE STREET, STRAND.

www.ingramcontent.com/pod-product-compliance
Lightning Source LLC
Chambersburg PA
CBHW032107220426
43664CB00008B/1168